Sacred Thinking
AWAKENING TO YOUR INNER POWER

"Sacred Thinking is an inclusive, empowering, engaging conversation about reality and the possibility for humanity."

- Tom Voccola, Author, The Accidental CEO,
A Leader's Journey from Ego to Purpose

"This extraordinary book is a true Godsend, as it gives us the understanding and awareness of the sacred power within each of us to create a life filled with abundant happiness, harmony and riches! Dr. Jim Lockard is one of the most important healers in our world today and Sacred Thinking opens our minds to the discovery of the treasures within our soul."

- Adrien Golday, Author, Regretland

Sacred Thinking

AWAKENING TO YOUR INNER POWER

JIM LOCKARD

OneSpirit Press
Simi Valley, California

Cover art by Bob Luckin
Cover Design by Frances Fujii

For information
OneSpirit@sbcglobal.net
OneSpirit Press books may be purchased for educational,
business, or sales promotion use.
For information, please contact: OneSpirit@sbcglobal.net

FIRST EDITION

Library of Congress Cataloging-in-Publication data

Lockard, James L. 1951–
SACRED THINKING, Awakening Your Inner Power/ James L. Lockard. – 1st
ed. Paperback includes appendix and index
ISBN: 978-0-557-11618-8
1. Spirituality 2. Religion 3. Self Help

Dedicated to my daughters

and greatest teachers:

Heather, Caitlyn, and Grace

And to honor my sweet daughter —

Caitlyn Erin Lockard

1990 ~ 2008

"You are the face of God . . ."

ACKNOWLEDGEMENTS

S*ACRED THINKING* represents much of what I have learned on my spiritual pathway over the past several decades. Since gratitude is both a spiritual practice and a causative agent, I would like to mention some of the people who have helped me to see myself at greater depth along the way, and whose wisdom is inextricably interwoven here. I cannot possibly include everyone – but I want to acknowledge the following people.

First of all, my wife and spiritual partner, Dorianne Cotter-Lockard, has been a constant source of inspiration and support. She helps me to look inside myself, to stay on track and has provided valuable insight and editing support for the book that you hold.

My formal teachers have been many, and include: Lou Tice, Bill Taliaferro, Arleen Bump, Edward Viljoen, Kathianne Lewis, and Knowlton Johnson. The most significant informal teachers: Barbara Marx Hubbard, Carlton Whitehead, Jack Richards, Robert Hitz, Candice Beckett, Kenn Gordon, Kennedy Schultz, Kathy Hearn, Jay Scott Neale, and David Walker.

The authors who lead me to significant new ideas, or who simply touched my heart: Ernest Holmes, Joseph Campbell, Wayne Dyer, Ken Wilber, Joseph Chilton Pearce, Marilyn Ferguson, Robert M. Pirsig, William Edelen, Thomas Troward, Andrew Harvey, Oriah Mountain Dreamer, Robert Bly, Rumi, Don Beck and Chris Cowan, Amit Goswami, Aldous Huxley, Debbie Ford, Carl Jung, Alan Watts, Ralph Waldo Emerson, Deepak Chopra, and Ralph Waldo Trine.

To those who helped in one way or another with this book: Stuart Goldfarb, Adrienne Golday, Candice Becket, Gayle Marchand, Todd Puntolillo, Dennis Merritt Jones, Ernie Chu, Lissa Coffey, Barbara Marx Hubbard, and Ellen Reid.

Special thanks to David Weitzman for his thoughtful editing assistance and to Tom Voccola and Frances Fujii for truly "above and beyond the call" design and editing to get the book ready for publication.

And to Bob Luckin for the amazing artwork on the cover – visit him and see his amazing work at **www.luckinart.com**.

TABLE OF CONTENTS

INTRODUCTION

There is more to you than you imagine. Whatever your problems, issues, or challenges, there is a connection within you, a connection with an Infinite Power – a connection that cannot be broken. What would your life be like if you knew – really knew – that you were connected to a divine power? If you really knew that you were never alone or separate – but connected at the deepest level with everyone and everything? Would that awareness change your life for the better?

You are a child of the Father – of the Father and the Mother God, the One Spirit. You contain the Christ Consciousness, the Light of the Spirit, the Buddha Mind, within you. And the Creator, however you conceive of this Power, *is* well pleased with you, loving you unconditionally by providing you with all that you need to live a happy and fulfilling life – requiring only that you use your intelligence to accept your good, not to turn away from it. The One Spirit is the Action of Life, the Animating Force within you and all of existence. Take joy in this. Let your mind entertain it and see how it feels to you. Listen to the wisdom of your heart. Choose to open to the Transcendent. It is there, waiting patiently.

There is nothing more important with respect to the way you experience life than your own beliefs about the nature of reality – all of reality, from the spiritual to the physical. You direct energy into your experience according to your belief system, which, for the most part, you have been building unconsciously as you have grown from an infant to an adult. One false belief leads to another, just as one true belief leads to another.

Your beliefs are created by your thinking – the words, images and feelings that make up your conscious thought process. When you use this creative process to build beliefs that bring you into greater alignment with Spirit-in-You, you are using Sacred Thinking.

SACRED THINKING is primarily based on a philosophy called New Thought. But it is more than a book on philosophy – my desire is to paint a word-picture of a new way of thinking about reality, a way that is growing rapidly in the minds of people everywhere. It is spiritually-based *and* grounded in logic and science. SACRED THINKING provides a structure to assist you in approaching reality; a structure that is useful in bringing about a new concept of yourself, a breaking away from the old false belief system, leading to one that is rewarding and positive.

Our 21st Century world is a place where access to knowledge is growing exponentially, where scientific inquiry and understanding provide a powerful source of awareness into the true nature of reality. At this time and place, the need for spirituality is greater than ever. When traditional religions are grounded in viewpoints based largely on worldviews that have been proven wrong and are outdated, outmoded, and potentially dangerous, a balance is required to keep peace among humanity. The approach in SACRED THINKING provides guideposts to this balanced view.

Humanity is currently struggling to find a way to integrate the wondrous discoveries of science and yet maintain a balanced spiritual viewpoint and the connection between the disciplines of science and spirituality. New Thought is the spearhead of a new spiritual viewpoint that allows for past, current, and future scientific discovery to exist harmoniously within an ever-expanding human consciousness, allowing for the integration of all systems of thought.

The New Thought movement in America has existed for more than a century, which is a relatively long time by American standards, but a very short time for the existence of a philosophy. It is a philosophy based upon some very ancient spiritual principles, yet it came of age during the age of scientific discovery. New Thought is unique among the world's philosophies in that it is equally compatible with ancient wisdom and modern science.

I have had countless people tell me, upon hearing New Thought principles for the first time, that it represents what they have always believed about reality, opening them to ideas and beliefs that existed below the surface of tradition and dogma.

One thing that makes New Thought unique, at least in the West, is a view of God or Spirit as an Infinite Presence and Power, with all of creation as Its expression. God is not viewed as a being living in a physical place called heaven, nor as a "force with a personality," but God AS everything – God as a tree, God as a solar system, God as the practice of medicine, and most importantly **God *as* you and me**. God as a continuously unfolding universe of expression, using evolution as Its means of coming into greater levels of being – God in you *and* you in God.

This viewpoint allows for an ***integral*** view of reality – one which includes all disciplines in a synergistic harmony. Most religions do not consider an integral view in their creeds, since they came into awareness at a time prior to the current level of human scientific understanding. Being grounded in earlier viewpoints of reality, these religious traditions have struggled with the new scientific discoveries of the current era. Every religion has a tendency to remain locked into the world-view of its earliest adherents. This, in turn, tends to create resistance and struggle with ever expanding breakthroughs in scientific discoveries. I believe that every great religion is true in its basic teachings – but not every interpretation of those teachings is true.

Modern science tells us that everything is part of a seamless fabric of energy, connected to everything else, within an intelligent self-organizing universe. New Thought acknowledges this, and adds the concept that each person (each individualized conscious being) within the universe commands intelligence, whether consciously or unconsciously, through which energy is directed into form and thereby co-creates individual experience.

The first section of this book discusses the nature of God or Spirit from a New Thought perspective – as an Infinite Spirit which infuses Its creation with Itself. The second section discusses some areas of study in the nature of reality as we understand them today. The final section presents an approach to spiritual practice that is about how to live your life in relationship to Spirit and to reality in a positive and fulfilling way – or an integral way, if you will. You may not agree with the viewpoints presented here – my suggestion is that you challenge any resistance you may be experiencing and consider whether the ideas make sense to you at a deep level.

I was raised as a Catholic, attended twelve years of Catholic school, went to church at least weekly, sometimes daily, thought about becoming a priest (very briefly, before I began to notice the girls), and lived in a family consisting of a few Catholics, quite a few Protestants, one agnostic (my Dad), and later on, some Jews. This upbringing brought me to a place of relative fear; fear about the world, my life, and about God. I could not see a way out of this fear, so I chose to ignore it. Upon graduation from Catholic (all boys) high school, I stopped attending church and did not return (except for weddings, funerals, and some ham and oyster suppers), until I was 38 years old.

I went to a New Thought community – The Science of Mind Center in Fort Lauderdale, Florida (now called the Center for Spiritual Living, Fort Lauderdale). There, I found a teaching and a worldview that connected with me in a deep way. It helped me to answer the questions that I asked the priests and nuns when I was 7 or 8 – questions that were not answered at all, or the answer was "it's a mystery," or "some questions should not be asked." I found many answers in the new teaching, but also many more questions. I have included some personal reflections in SACRED THINKING, which you may read or simply skip over as you choose.

I wrote SACRED THINKING to bring New Thought principles to a broader audience, and have included other materials which are compatible with, yet not traditionally a part of, New Thought. This allows you to understand a philosophy and theology which embraces the full range of human understanding and experience, and which promotes growth with respect to the ever expanding nature of that understanding and experience. My invitation is to read SACRED THINKING with "new eyes," setting aside your current beliefs – as much as possible – and then evaluate the book based on how you resonate or connect with its contents. If the concepts resonate with you, please apply them in your life in order to irrefutably prove their truth.

Our spiritual identity co-exists and creates the platform from which we view external reality. We need a spiritual perspective to help us to use our new technologies wisely. We need to be free to explore the frontiers of science without being limited by old worldviews and limited, fear based concepts which tend to stifle growth and constrain the expression of what is possible.

You and I are a part of a great and powerful universal expression, and it is time that we, along with humanity as a whole, awaken to this truth.

Some Beliefs Upon Which This Book Is Based

1.   **There is ONE Infinite Spirit. This One Spirit created the universe out of Itself, out of Its own infinite nature.** It is the ground of all being and everything that exists is part of It. Being infinite, It can never be fully comprehended by any individual human being or all human beings as a collective. This Spirit, and aspects of It, has been given many names. If there are "lesser gods," they are within the One Spirit. The simplest definition of this One Spirit is "Love."

2.   **The universe, or cosmos, is the expression of the creative nature of the One Spirit.** The universe that you know and any other universes which may exist are all part of the One Spirit. Because of the Infinite Nature of this One Spirit, nothing can exist outside it; nothing can exist apart from It. Everything that exists has its being within the One Spirit.

3.   **The Universe is constantly changing, moving toward greater and greater complexity.** This is done through a process called evolution, which has been going on at least since the Big Bang – our name for the origin of the universe. Evolution appears to be a process through which Spirit manifests increasing degrees of complexity and intelligence in Its creation. As of now, human beings exist at the pinnacle of evolution, so far as is known. It can be said that greater intelligence *emerges* from potential to actualization by means of evolution. Human beings have reached a point in our evolutionary development where we can and do consciously affect the process of evolution.

4.   **The Universe and everything in it is infused with intelligence and is self-organizing.** Behind every thing is an invisible Power, a Power that is the Ground of All Being, and The Animating Force. This Power expresses as the physical or manifest universe and the energy therein. This Power expresses impersonally

– it is fully available to all.

5. **As a human being, you are an individualized (not individual, which means separate) expression of the One Spirit, as are all other human beings and everything else in creation.** You can never be separate from Spirit, nor can you ever truly be separate from anything else in creation. Your connection to everything is invisible, consisting of energy (both physical and non-physical) and intelligence. Your intelligence, your mind, is part of the Mind (Spirit) which created everything.

6. **Spirit experiences being human by means of you and all other human beings.** This experience is not *through* you but *as* you. Spirit does the same thing with all levels and beings of creation. Why Spirit does this is a mystery that is ultimately unknowable.

7. **Within each human being is the potential to fully experience the connection with the One Spirit.** A number of great spiritual teachers have set examples as to how this can be done. The collective human consciousness is, it seems, poised on the verge of emerging into the level of awareness necessary to experience this connection on a mass level. Each of us possesses a mind that is the locus of our experience of reality, of life experiences. Our thoughts create our mental images and beliefs. Sacred Thinking creates a mindset that connects with Spirit in a way that can bring bliss, connection, harmony, and empowerment. Right now, a relative few have done the preparatory work through spiritual practices to move into this new awareness. Human beings have reached an evolutionary point where the choice can be made to seek this awareness. Will you make that choice?

SACRED THINKING
AWAKENING TO YOUR INNER POWER

SACRED THINKING

"The world is saturated with Divinity, immersed in Reality, and filled with Possibility. We must take this Divine Possibility and mold it into present Actuality in everyday experience. This is the way to freedom, the pathway to peace and happiness."
~ *Ernest Holmes*

"It is enough for me to contemplate the mystery of conscious life, perpetuating itself through all eternity; to reflect upon the marvelous structure of the Universe; and to try humbly to comprehend even an infinitesimal part of the intelligence manifested in nature."
~ *Albert Einstein*

PART ONE:

THE NATURE OF GOD, THE ONE INFINITE SPIRIT

"SPIRIT: God, within Whom all spirits exist. The Self-Knowing One. The Conscious Universe. The Absolute. Spirit in man is that part of him which enables him to know himself. . . . We define Spirit as First Cause, or God; the Universal I AM. The Spirit is Self propelling, It is All; It is Self-Existent and has all life within Itself. It is the Word and the Word is volition. It is Will because It chooses. It is Free Spirit because It knows nothing outside Itself, and nothing different from Itself. Spirit is the Father/Mother God because It is the Principle of Unity back of all things. Spirit is all Life, Truth, Love, Being, Cause and Effect, and is the only Power in the Universe that knows Itself."

~ Ernest Holmes, THE SCIENCE OF MIND, Glossary

Chapter One

ORIGINS

"In the beginning, God . . ."
~ THE HOLY BIBLE, Genesis 1:1

nd the trouble begins . . . for the human mind is normally trapped in limitations. What is the trouble? The trouble of how to handle competing definitions and limited beliefs regarding an Infinite God that can never fully be defined. The trouble of individuals and religious institutions promoting separation based on these limited definitions. The best one can do is to define It[1] in a limited way, which means that someone else will perhaps define It in an equally limited, but potentially different way. Each will declare his own definition complete and true. Then someone else will define It another way, again equally limited, and declare that definition complete and true. Each will then declare the other two to be heretics, and then war will follow. Such has been the history of humanity.

"Behold but One in all things; it is the second that leads you astray."
~ Kabir

"How transcendent and immaculate is God!
He has neither place, nor time, nor beginning, nor temporal continuity, nor
posterior eternity, nor temporal priority, nor terminal end, and yet all the while,
He is neither occupied with, nor seeks succor from,
that which He has brought into being." ~ Shibli in Sarraj Tusi

---

[1] I use the word "It" for God, or The One Spirit, instead of the more common "He," because as an infinite reality, The One Spirit encompasses all that is masculine and all that is feminine. Actually, using "He" as a descriptor is limiting. "It" is meant as a more inclusive term, not as a diminutive.

The trouble can only be avoided if one understands that whatever definition of Spirit one comes to believe, something will be missing – and that missing "something" is itself infinite reality. I cannot get close to the complete truth of the One Spirit with my limited intellect; I believe no one can. I can only create some definition that is greater than I am and work from there, all the while realizing that there is much more – infinitely more. I must allow that others will have different definitions, which, while different from mine, may well be equally or even more true, without devaluing my own definition.

"If" you and I can allow that, we can live in peace.

That's a big "if."

Perhaps the first thing I need to address to honor the "if" is to develop the quality of *humility*. Humility is not about putting me down; it is about seeing things from a truthful position. Humility is about allowing life to unfold without having to condemn or judge it. I simply cannot comprehend an infinite with my human intellect. I can, however, comprehend aspects of the infinite. The One Spirit is the infinite reality. So I seek the grandest most elegant definition I can, and then I keep expanding upon it as I grow in awareness and deepen my practices, all the while realizing that I will NEVER get to the point where that definition cannot be expanded or deepened. I need to be okay with this process. That is the humility I am talking about. Can you imagine that? Can you manage that?

Can you do what I am suggesting even though you may be a Christian, Buddhist, Taoist, Muslim, Jew, Zoroastrian, Wiccan, New Ager, Religious Scientist, Shinto, Navajo, or the follower of any other (or no) religious teaching? I challenge you, as I challenge myself, to practice this type of humility.

The ultimate goal in this work is more than an intellectual understanding of One Spirit – the goal is rather a complete identity with One Spirit – a *merging*, as the Sufis say, into the Beloved One. It is a merging so complete that the self is lost, yet the gain is paradoxically infinite and immeasurable. Greater understanding of One Spirit automatically comes as we humbly open our minds and hearts and our awareness rises.

> *"It's no good asking for a simple religion."*
> ~ C.S. Lewis

> *"Belief is the lowest form of religious involvement, and, in fact, it often seems to operate with no authentic religious connection whatsoever. The 'true believer'* . . . *embraces a more-or-less codified belief system that appears to act most basically as a fund of immortality symbols."*
> ~ Ken Wilbur, SENSE AND SOUL

Can you engage in blind faith in a world that is now increasingly technological, materialistic, and scientific, where linear thinking is the norm and symbolic or metaphorical thinking has been diminished and devalued? Can you do it in a world where religion itself seems increasingly unnecessary, outdated and outstripped, sometimes even destructive? A world where the religious institutions seem to be losing their grip, unraveling, and reacting with increasing conservatism, dogmatism, even violence, over fear of losing the battle of whose definition of God or Spirit reigns supreme?

That's a good question.

If God is more than any, or even all of us can imagine, why would you blindly follow the teachings of any individual or group of people who give what **has to be** a limited viewpoint of the Divine? Can you learn to trust your heart, your intuitive wisdom, to lead you to the highest truth for you? Can you deepen your realization of your own spiritual nature, and look to express love and kindness in your life?

Maybe what we need is a new beginning.

"All that is in heaven and earth gives glory to Allah.
He is the Mighty, the Wise One.
His is the kingdom of the heavens and the earth.
He ordains life and death and has power over all things.
He is the first and the last, the visible and the unseen.
He has knowledge of all things.
He created the heavens and the earth in six days
and then mounted His throne.
He knows all that goes into the earth
and all that emerges from it,
all that comes down from heaven and all that ascends to it.
He is with you wherever you are.
He is cognizant of all your actions.
His is the kingdom of the heavens and the earth.
To Him shall all things return.
He causes the night to pass into the day and the day into the night.
He has knowledge of the inmost thoughts of men."
~ THE QUR'AN, 57:1

SPIRITUAL PRACTICE

Throughout this book, I will be suggesting various spiritual practices to supplement the information provided with the expectation that a change in awareness will come if you humbly engage in the practice.

Sit quietly and close your eyes. Allow the idea or your definition of God, of Spirit to come to your mind and your heart. What image or images arise in your consciousness?

- What does the image say about your idea of God?

- Does the image feel kind and loving?

- Does it feel harsh and judgmental?

- A bit of both?

Write out your images. Ponder them. Let them sink in. You may not have thought about this subject for some time. In order to open your mind – which of course is the goal of this exercise – you must be able to identify your idea of God. You must identify your starting point.

- Next, read this chapter again from the viewpoint of your newly revitalized image of God or Spirit. See if anything has changed.

Chapter Two

DEFINING GOD

"Be still and know I am GOD. I will be exalted among the heathen.
I will be exalted in the Earth."
~ THE HOLY BIBLE, Psalm 46:10

A definition of God which can bring a greater degree of meaning, reverence, and relevance to a wider group of people with diverse cultural, ethnic, and national backgrounds would be a wonderful development. Defining God is an essential starting point if we are to move away from limited, dogmatic thinking. There are three things you want to consider when defining God:

1) Each religion has many suggested guidelines for you to use in this process.

2) Your definition of God will, by necessity, be unique to you. No matter how closely you may try to adhere to an existing definition of God as set forth by a teacher or an organization, it is inevitable that you personalize it to some degree. This is actually a good thing. Become your own authority in defining God!

3) No true spiritual teacher who has developed a well accepted definition of God used a pre-existing definition, except as a starting point. Most are original definitions and tend to "include and transcend" what has come before.

"With sincerity and earnestness one can realize God through all religions.
The Vaishnavas will realize God, and so will the Saktas, the Vedantists,
and the Brahmos. The Mussalmans and Christians will realize Him too.
All will certainly realize God if they are earnest and sincere."
~ Sri Ramakrishna

By the way, you already have a definition of God, whether you consciously decided to create one or not. You use your subconscious sense of this definition as you make moment to moment decisions about the nature of things and the choices you make about your behavior. Your idea of God, your image, is so completely intertwined with your subconscious mind that you may rarely even think about it. Your definition operates automatically, and has been built from everything that you have taken in up until this very moment. Most of us live our lives after reaching a certain age with a fixed idea about God, and it is through this filter that we interpret and give meaning to God and the world around us.

So stop and ask yourself these questions:

- What is my definition of God?

- Does my God have form? What image have I given God?

- What feelings does this idea of God evoke within me?

- How is this concept of God working for or against me in my life?

> *"The knower and the known are one. Simple people imagine*
> *that they should see God as if He stood there and they here.*
> *This is not so. God and I, we are one in knowledge."*
> ~ Meister Eckhart

From the broadest possible perspective, God is infinite. So we begin with that idea, the infinite nature of God, and then look at what next seems intelligent and loving. I believe that the best way to approach any problem waiting for solution is from the most intelligent and loving position that one can express at any given moment – your wisest and best. When you can do that on a regular basis from a consciousness of love and empowerment, you are living from your authentic center!

"Who is God? I can think of no better answer than, He who is. Nothing is more appropriate to the eternity which God is. If you call God good, or great, or blessed, or wise, or anything else of this sort, it is included in these words, namely, He is."
~ St. Bernard

"Spirit – God, within whom all spirits exist. The Self-Knowing One. The Conscious Universe. The Absolute. Spirit in man is that part of him which enables him to know himself. That which he really is. . . . We define Spirit as the First Cause or God; the Universal I AM. The Spirit is Self-Propelling, It is All; It is Self-Existent and has all life within Itself. It is the Word and the Word is volition. . . . It knows nothing outside Itself, and nothing different from Itself. Spirit is the Father-Mother God because It is the Principle of Unity back of all things. Spirit is all Life, Truth, Love, Being, Cause and Effect, and is the only Power in the Universe that knows Itself."
~ Ernest Holmes

An Infinite God must contain all possibilities, including qualities of potential that are not loving or intelligent. When you experience those negative qualities, you are not apart from God, more accurately, you are out of harmony with your higher potentialities. Of course, this occurs only when you choose[2] them. It seems to me that human beings are born with natural urges toward love and wisdom. We do not always realize life experiences that are consistent with love and wisdom, to be sure, but it is always there as a desire and usually this desire comes into your goals and dreams. You want your definition of God to support you in being your best, so wisdom and love are good qualities to begin with.

"But O how wonderful!
I am the unbounded deep
In whom all living things

---

[2] The choice may be actively conscious, or it may be unconscious in the sense that it conforms to the natural flow of thoughts arising from your own beliefs – either is actually a choice.

Naturally arise,
Rush against each other playfully,
And then subside."
~ Ashtavakra Gita 2:25

We look to God as the One Source of all energy and creation, the Ground of All Being. Your life is from God; your intelligence is from God. You are part of God – again, since God is infinite, nothing can be separate from God, you included. Nothing, not you, not anyone or anything, can be outside of the infinite. And therefore, if God is infinite, then you and all of creation are part of God, within God. That is also a humble statement, don't you think?

BE STILL AND KNOW

"Be still and know that I am God." This quote from Psalms in the Holy Bible has been used to identify oneself with God, as being a part of God. I AM God, just not all of what God is. I AM God, just as every atom is God. Every breath is God, every rock is God, and every fish is God. This idea does not diminish God, as no idea can diminish the infinite, but it expands the idea of God to something grander, more personal, more integral to Its creation, of which we are all a part.

The quote begins with the command, *"Be still,"* recognition that the idea of God is best recognized from within, in a state of quiet solitude. A mystic is one who is comfortable with the inner self and learns to *be still*. Stillness is a quality that must be cultivated, usually through the practice of meditation, to know the magnificent extent of the divinity within you on a continual basis.

The rest of the quote, *"I will be exalted among the heathen. I will be exalted in the earth,"* has often been interpreted in a divisive way. If you see the "heathen" merely as someone who has formed a very limited, or simply different, definition of God, rather than as someone who is against some "true" doctrine, then it can be seen differently and less divisively. be exalted among the heathen and in the earth can also be interpreted to mean that God is all there is. The heathen is part of God, the earth is part of God, and it's all God – simple, pure, inclusive of all, no division.

". . . in the Chandogya Upanishad, the key word to such a meditation is announced: **tat tvam asi,** *'Thou art that,' or "You yourself are It!' The final sense of a religion such as Hinduism or Buddhism is to bring about in the individual an experience, one way or another, of his own identity with that mystery that is the mystery of all being."*
~ Joseph Campbell

I believe that all religions have correctly set forth the true reason for human experience: to live a full life and to recall a conscious experience of one's Spirit Nature. That's it. When a faith tradition goes beyond this, it tends to diverge into all sorts of other areas of belief, ritual and dogma. Some of this is about living in the physical and emotional world, some of it is soothing, some is inspirational, but little of it is really essential to experience your own Spirit Nature.

Science, primarily through the field of quantum physics, is beginning to get better at understanding the nature of the mystery of God or Life. Science is exploring the nature of how the manifest universe relates to Spirit and how Sprit relates to the manifest universe. Other than this, not much has changed regarding our understanding of God since ancient times. In fact, it seems that we have recently become bored with the quest for our Spirit-Natures, focusing our attention and efforts on building nations, cities, and technology. These diversions have become our gods; the mall, the sports stadium and our houses of worship. Churches and synagogues seem almost quaint by comparison; not the place where one goes to reconnect to primary energy, but instead a place of solace or obligation.

The tallest building in the city is no longer the church or temple; it is the financial building – money being more attractive than the version of God being presented by the churches. Next in height come the government buildings – power being more attractive than that version of God being presented by the churches, and also easier to come by.

Is this a good thing or a bad thing?

THERE ARE NO BAD THINGS

There are no bad things; there are no good things. That is a function of human belief alone. There are just things to which we give meaning.

"Man is made by his belief. As he believes, so he is."
~ Bhagavad-Gita

"There is nothing either good or bad, but thinking makes it so".
~ Shakespeare, (Hamlet, Act II, Scene II)

"It is mind which gives to things their quality, their foundation and their being. Whoever speaks or acts with impure mind, him sorrow follows, as the wheel follows the steps of the ox that draws the cart."
~ The Dhammapada

The ancients of both east and west tell us that God is good, that creation is good, that it is all good. The words God and good have the same root – they therefore carry the same meaning. The creation stories, the myths that represent the beliefs of a culture as to its connection to God, all show an affirmative Spirit creating a good world or universe. Then man and woman, using unique free will combined with our intelligence, make choices that represent the ability to make life difficult and sad, even tragic. How? We did this by being ignorant and/or in fear because we misunderstood our true nature – and then, there we are in the game of life. When we apply intelligent awareness and love to our worldviews, we co-create something joyful and magnificent with our lives and our cultures.

*"Then God saw everything that He had made, and indeed **it was** very good.*
So the evening and the morning were the sixth day."
~ THE HOLY BIBLE, Genesis, 1:31

"We are the guests of an invisible Host whose presence we feel and whose form
we shall see when our eyes are opened to the fact that It clothes Itself in
innumerable forms. It is our business to unite, not to divide; to include, not to
exclude; to accept, and not to renounce."
~ Ernest Holmes

Another essential quality which should be a part of your definition of God is "unity." But wait. If God is good and creation is good, how can what creation does be bad? Maybe what we identify as bad is simply a secondary means by which we learn and grow. Did you ever need something to go wrong in your life before you would pay attention? Did you ever have someone leave you, only to then realize that you needed change to occur to continue to grow and flourish? Have you ever really learned to live because someone close to you died? Did you ever notice how your life makes sense when you look into the past, but seems chaotic when looking into the future? Do you ever think there might be a pattern here? Could this pattern be meaningful? If it is all good, then maybe you are all good, too. Can you believe that? Maybe the world is now ready to awaken to something known at deeper levels. A world where there is One Power, not two.

"Behold the words of the Qur'an:
'We are closer to you than you are yourself.'
Comprehend your relationship with God!
He is closer to us than our own selves.
Yet through ignorance we search for Him wandering from door to door."
~ Sufi poem
"I am neither the mind, the intellect, nor the silent voice within;
Neither the eyes, the ears, the nose, nor the mouth.
I am not water, fire, earth, nor ether — I am Consciousness and Bliss.
I am Shiva! I am Shiva!"
~ Shankaracharya

I will close this chapter on the definition of God with the use of a different word for the name of the Creative Intelligence. The word "God" is laden with so many meanings for so many people, and many of those definitions are limiting and fear-based. When we fear God, what we fear is a God of limited definition created thousands of years ago. We also cannot help but project our own limited qualities onto our self-created image of God. When we know this, we are best served by creating a higher definition, a more magnificent image of God, not merely of a loving God, but of a God that IS Love and only Love.

The feeling that I experience when I view God in this way, as Love and nothing else, is one of great joy and possibility. I hope and trust that it will be the same with you. Rather than fearing a wrathful deity who is the creation of the projection of human fears, you create a loving and enduring Creative Force that is pure potential, pure love, and pure joy.

So I will use the words "Spirit" or "The One Spirit" or "Infinite Spirit" in the rest of this book instead of God. It means the same thing, but may have a new and different feeling for those readers who feel bound in some way by the word "God."

Of course, you can use any word you like in your own thoughts. I trust you will find one or more that gives rise to joy, love, and wisdom within you.

SPIRITUAL PRACTICE

- On a sheet of paper, draw a horizontal line dividing it into two equal halves. At the top, put your favorite name for Spirit. Put that name just below the horizontal line as well.

- On the bottom half of the page, list the qualities and attributes of Spirit (it might include things like: Infinite, Love, Power, Truth, accepting, compassionate, affirmative, etc.).

- On the top half of the page, make a drawing that depicts your idea of Spirit – there is no wrong way to do this.

- Add to the top and the bottom of the page from time to time as your definition changes. If appropriate, create a new sheet when your definition has major changes.

- On a separate sheet, draw the horizontal line. Put YOUR name at the top of each section.

- On the bottom half, list YOUR qualities that are divine. Put a score of 1 to 10 next to each, 10 being highest. Decide to work on the qualities that have lower scores.

- On the top half, draw yourself as the most ideal version of YOU that you can be.

- Add to the top and the bottom of the page from time to time as your definition changes. If appropriate, create a new sheet when your definition has major changes.

PERSONAL REFLECTION

My mother kept a small ceramic statue of the Madonna on her dresser or her night table in her bedroom. It was painted with blue trim and the head of the Madonna was covered with a cloth and tilted softly to the side.

For some reason, this became the basis for my image of God as a small child. I saw God as masculine, as instructed, and in my imagination created a grayscale version of this statue with a slightly more androgynous face. It was no longer clearly feminine, and not purely masculine. For some reason, this worked for me, perhaps because my mother was the parent whom I saw as most godlike.

Being a young Catholic on the east coast in the 1950's was a very powerful experience. Joseph Campbell wrote and spoke often of his Catholic upbringing in an earlier decade. The effect of the mythology – the stories, the symbols, the magical nature of heaven, and God, the angels, and Lucifer, were captivating. The seeming conflict between the angry God and the loving God put me into an intense inner conflict about how to resolve this paradox and make sense of the world around me in light of that resolution.

Childhood was an intense religious time, where I struggled with the apparent inconsistencies between life as I saw it lived around me, and the strict admonitions of the church that were constantly spoken from the front of the classroom and the pulpit. I would not say that I felt very comforted by my religious instruction, but it did provide a sense of order to my world.

Chapter Three

THE VOID AND THE FIELD

"In the beginning
There was neither existence nor non-existence,
All this world was manifest energy . . .
The One breathed, without breath, by Its own power
Nothing else was there . . ."
~ Hymn of Creation, The Rig Veda

Thu Void is another name I will use for that aspect of The One Spirit which is pure Spirit. It represents the nothingness out of which all things arise, and back into which all things must go, also called The Unmanifest.

"In the beginning God created the heavens and the earth.
The earth was without form, and void; and darkness was on the face of the deep.
And the Spirit of God was hovering over the face of the waters.
Then God said, 'Let there be light"; and there was light.
And God saw the light, that it was good;
and God divided the light from the darkness."
~ THE HOLY BIBLE, Genesis, Chapter 1:1 – 2

What is the cause of the cosmos? Is it Brahman?
From where do we come? By what life?
Where shall we find peace at last?
What power governs the duality
Of pleasure and pain by which we are driven?
Time, nature, necessity, accident,
Elements, energy, intelligence--
None of these can be the First Cause.
They are effects, whose only purpose is
To help the self rise above pleasure and pain.
~ Shvetashvatara Upanishad

The Field is the expression of the Void. The Field is the

manifest universe – a Field of pure energy and intelligence. The Field is totally within the Void; but the Void is only partially in the Field. The Field is the dance floor – where the action is. You are a part of both the Field and the Void. And you dance.

While this interplay between the Void and the Field may seem a strange idea, it comes out of the recent awakening of modern technological science and its understanding of the quantum nature of reality. It is a joining of modern science, for the first time, with much of ancient spiritual wisdom or, at least it is a beginning of such an integration. Many resist this viewpoint, however, truth is always resisted when it is initially uncovered. This also does not mean that what is resisted is always the truth, but it does mean that we may want to keep an open mind.

"Jesus said: The seeker should not stop until he finds. When he does find, he will be disturbed. After having been disturbed, he will be astonished. Then he will reign over everything."
~ The Gospel of Thomas, Saying 2

THE FIELD IS SUPPORTED BY INTELLIGENCE

The Field by necessity must be supported by something. Quantum physicists have described a thin layer of intelligence underlying the quantum field (the quantum, or zero-point, field is defined as all of the energy in existence). This intelligence, seen from the universal level or the macrocosm, can be called "Universal Intelligence" or The One Spirit. Seen from any lesser level (collective, or individual, or microcosmic), it is consciousness.

Consciousness, which is intelligence, is an organizing force in the manifest universe. Consciousness takes raw energy and organizes it. This organized energy becomes something in the manifest universe – a planet or star, an atom, water, a human being, a feeling or an experience.

You are organized energy, some of it in the form of matter,

drawn together by the intelligence within you and around you. The intelligence within and around you is part of the intelligence of The One Spirit.

When you think about it, what else could it be?

There is only The One Spirit, nothing else. Nothing can exist outside of the Infinite One Spirit. You are part of the Divine Infinite, the part that is designed to be one human being – you. To be sure, you interact and are part of the larger field of consciousness called humanity, and the even larger field called life, and the larger field called the universe. But no matter where you divide it, you are part of the Mind of The One Spirit – your mind is an aspect of The One Spirit's Mind – and, therefore, all divisions are illusions.

"The Beloved is in all; the lover merely veils Him;
The Beloved is all that lives, the lover a dead thing."
~ Jalaludin Rumi

The key to co-creating a harmonious life is to use your mind intelligently, in harmony with all of the power within you. If Spirit is infinite, and all of creation is in Spirit, and Spirit created you, then you have to be in Spirit and part of Spirit and of the nature of Spirit. How could you not be of the nature of your Creator? How could you be alien to that which created you?

Finding and relating to one's true spiritual nature has been the purpose of every major religion. This has often been defined as following the "will" of a deity as determined by some person or group of people. Or setting your selfhood aside and living in some form of deprivation as sacrifice, or journeying outside of your self to seek wisdom from afar.. When we think of this in terms of oneness, we see that there is no separation – that our perception of separation is ultimately an illusion. Everyone and everything is connected – we live in a universe of interrelationships, of unity.

"We arrive at a consciousness of Unity only in such degree as we see that what we are looking FOR, we are looking WITH and looking AT."
~ Ernest Holmes, THE SCIENCE OF MIND

Suppose that The One Spirit is within you and within me right here and now? Suppose the true journey is inward, to the deepest part of self. Suppose that that is what the great spiritual teachers have been saying all along, often in symbolic terms? Suppose, for example, that the Ascension of Jesus was not actually "upward" toward a physical heaven, but inward, toward perfect realization of his true Christ-Nature? What if each of us has that Christ-Nature as our true immutable potential as well?

If that is so, and I believe it is, then it would explain numerous inconsistencies, and we could come to see Jesus as the Great Example, rather than the Great Exception. The imitation of Christ would take on greater, more attainable meaning as we see him as equally divine with all other living souls, but with a greater, yet attainable, degree of realization of this truth. The Christ is in you every bit as much as within him. Jesus the man simply recognized this great truth, as can you!

THE NATURE OF ENERGY

The Field arises out of the Void and contains all of the actualized energy that exists. As consciousness acts, some of the energy begins to resonate at different frequencies as directed by that consciousness. Energy is directed or organized into form and begins to act like all of the forces and things in the universe, as intelligence acts upon it.

The Void contains both "potential" and "actualized" energy. This means that all things which are possible already exist as "potential". Again, since The One Spirit is infinite, and you cannot add anything to the infinite, all possibilities **must** exist in a field of pure potential. This potential becomes actualized, that is, it comes into expression in the Field, by means of intelligent choice. Your intelligence is a part of the choice-making intelligence which actualizes potential into form. You are part of the Mind of Spirit and that is your nature – to co-create as an aspect of God.

As Deepak Chopra has written, you are essentially a "disturbance" in the Field. You are a disturbance in the sense that the individualized portion of Divine Intelligence that you are acts on the energy in its close proximity and draws to itself what is needed to create your form and experience. You are a self-organizing mechanism, constantly exchanging energy with your surroundings, constantly communicating with the rest of the universe in a two-way conversation of energy impulses. The intelligence that is you creates a "disturbance" in what would otherwise be a flat, uniform field of energy. Very dynamic, isn't it?

"The most beautiful and most profound religious emotion that we can experience is the sensation of the mystical. And this mysticality is the power of all true science. If there is such a concept as God, it is a Subtle Spirit, not an image of a man that so many have fixed in their minds. In essence, my religion consists of a humble admiration for this illimitable superior spirit that reveals itself in the slight details that we are able to perceive with our frail and feeble minds."
~ Albert Einstein

What is happening is that The One Spirit is having conversations with and relating to Itself. You are an individualized aspect of The One Spirit, rather than an individual. Like the fingers on your hand, which could not function if removed from the rest of the hand, you could not function if removed from the Divine Consciousness. Of course, you could not be removed from the Divine Consciousness, because that would make you separate from the One Spirit, which an impossibility.

This idea of you as an individualization *of* the One Spirit rather than an individual *from* the One Spirit is critical because it means that any sense that you are separate from your surroundings is an illusion. It is as if your right index finger believed that it was not connected to the same hand as your right thumb. This belief in separation is what creates all of your problems and all of the problems of humanity.

You live in both the Void and the Field. You are a transitory being (with an infinite soul) with connections to both Spirit and Spirit-As-Form. You are able to bring new things into expression by using your creative mind. All of your spiritual growth depends on how you embody this information and how you act upon it from this new realization.

SPIRITUAL PRACTICE

- Sit quietly and close your eyes. Imagine yourself in the vastness of space surrounded by distant stars and galaxies stretching ever outward toward infinity and beyond. See if you can feel your connection to all this vastness of infinite space and time.

- Next imagine yourself as an electron floating around the nucleus of an atom. See if you can feel your connection to the smallest of things while feeling the connection with the vastness of space.

- Finally, search to feel the presence of Spirit in the vastness and in the smallness. Let yourself experience this for several minutes, then journal about it and see what comes to you.

Chapter Four

SPIRIT WITHIN YOU - YOU WITHIN SPIRIT

"Humankind is being led along an evolving course,
Through this migration of intelligences,
And though we seem to be sleeping,
There is an inner wakefulness
That directs the dream,
And that will eventually startle us back
To the truth of who we are."
~ Rumi

The inner wakefulness of which the mystical Sufi poet Jalaludin Rumi writes is the Divine Consciousness as both the collective and the individualized wisdom that pervades all of creation. This is sometimes described as the Watcher or the Witness. Creation, the manifest universe, or The Field, might be defined as energy activated and organized (or actualized) by intelligence. This intelligence operates at the macrocosmic and microcosmic levels. Science has shown us that everything in the manifest universe is made of the same stuff – organized energy. Spiritual wisdom has told us this for thousands of years.

"Be humble for you are made of earth. Be noble for you are made of stars."
~ Serbian Proverb.

Spirit's purpose seems to be creation – to bring forth or manifest that which is unmanifest in the Mind of Infinite Spirit. Evolution is the process of creation, governed by law, or principle, driven by intelligence and valuing spontaneity. The evolutionist and the creationist each have a piece of the truth in understanding the process of creation. First is the idea in the Mind of God, and then the manifestation of the idea following the laws of physics.

At the individualized human level, it is often impossible to understand the process of creation clearly, so massive and powerful is the Universal Mind. And yet, you can discern aspects of It, patterns of action that make sense to you, for you are made of It and are of Its nature. That which you are looking for, you are looking with, as Ernest Holmes said. There is an inherent connection that forms the subtext for all of your experience, which, of course, is the Universal Mind of Spirit.

"We do not move toward God by understanding. As long as we cling to what we can understand, imagine, or even desire, especially as long as we depend on our own efforts, we will not reach God, who transcends all that we are, all that we can achieve. We must move from knowing to unknowing, from daylight to the night of faith. Our spiritual ascent is a journey by night. Faith is our only light. Therefore we must begin our ascent to God with minds and souls emptied of whatever images, whatever ideas of him have come through our senses. The light of faith does not improve our human intellect; it overwhelms it."
~ St. John of the Cross

Do you not learn best about The One Spirit by discovering more about yourself?

Where else would one look is a better question. Can someone else, themselves individualized and limited, lead you to Spirit? Can someone else give you your own truth? Or is your experience of the world around you really a projection of your own inner beliefs and feelings about yourself and your relationship to the world around you?

"A fool sees himself as another, but a wise man sees others as himself."
~ Zen patriarch Dogen (1200-1253)

So you try to understand The Field, of which you are a part, from the standpoint of your own nature, which you have greatly misunderstood. It is like a fish trying to understand water – can she even notice it? If she notices it, can she ever understand it if she sees it as separate from herself? Does she realize that she is over 90% water herself?

Can you get a clear understanding of The Field if you begin by believing in separation? If unity is the fundamental nature of being, does that not change the basic way that you understand yourself and your existence within The Field (which exists within The Void, which is the Ground of All Being)? If your mind is within the Universal Mind, what does that say about how you can understand the Universal Mind and your relationship to It?

> *"Nobody has yet invented a Spiritual Calculus, in terms of which we may talk coherently about the divine Ground and of the world conceived as its manifestation."*
> ~ Aldous Huxley, THE PERENNIAL PHILOSOPHY

Perhaps that "Spiritual Calculus" is emerging today. It is coming from the gradual acceptance of some of the ideas of quantum physics (and whatever will follow quantum physics) into everyday understanding. I would say that a society tends to be about 100 to 150 years behind its leading scientists in understanding the nature of reality. That is, most of western society is still living in a Newtonian world, seeing everything as separate and mechanical, a view which has some validity, but is ultimately limited.

Quantum physics, now about 100 years old, is beginning to have a more widespread level of recognition today. Of course, this comes with a high degree of resistance and misunderstanding which accompanies any major shift in understanding. The identical phenomenon occurred when the change took place from an essentially mythical/magical world view to the "scientific" world view of Newtonian/Cartesian physics. The current quantum worldview expands our ability to understand the universe and ourselves at a deeper level; what any paradigm shift does. Our awareness expands to understand it at a deeper and/or broader level. We can use this awareness to expand our experience of life.

I should point out that I do not believe that quantum physics is able to explain anything significant in the mystical realm. Quantum physics is a scientific discipline that describes the physical level of nature, and any repeated attempts to make this discipline fit various ideas about mysticism, or even mind-in-action, are questionable, in my opinion. I am in agreement with philosopher Ken Wilber, who points out the failure of quantum physics to resolve questions about non-physical aspects of reality.

The move away from Newtonian physics toward something less predictable yet more intelligent and conscious is also, paradoxically, a move back toward the ancient wisdom traditions. However, the route through the Newtonian viewpoint and the scientific revolution has been very positive, as it has taken us (potentially, at least) beyond a purely mythical/magical and superstitious view of reality toward a more practical understanding of a universe that has a distinct mystical/spiritual grounding. As a result of this experience, we become a species on the brink of becoming capable of practical living in a universe that we realize is first mysterious in a quantum sense, and also predictable and practical in a Newtonian sense.

*"Quantum transformation is nature's tradition. . . . The jump from pre-life to life, or from the most intelligent animal to early human is an example of quantum transformation. The creation of radical newness is an evolutionary fact. Once there was no Earth, then there was Earth. Once there was no life, then life appeared. Once there was no biosphere and then the whole living Earth blossomed forth. Once there were no humans, and then we emerged. We learn to expect the unexpected and anticipate the new, and discover that what is 'natural' is to innovate and transform when reaching a limit. Nature has been transcending for billions of years, and now we, through our evolving **human** nature are participating in the process consciously for the first time."*
~ Barbara Marx Hubbard

Some will move into this new paradigm sooner, some later, and some will simply not do so at all. These levels of understanding are already showing up in the larger culture. The difference today is that the rate of change is gaining speed, and it is much more likely that one will fall behind the leading edge of human discovery. Another effect of this increased rate of change is that the "trailing edge" and the middle levels of development get farther behind the "leading edge" of human awareness. The rise of fundamentalism as a world phenomenon in the last century and a half is one effect of this increasing rate of change. Fundamentalism is the "digging in of heels" when people resist what they perceive as too much change too quickly, threatening a worldview which was thought to be stable.

The consciousness of humanity is spiraling toward greater and greater complexity at an increasing rate. Never before has change in human knowledge happened so rapidly on this planet. There are more and more complex levels of awareness emerging and co-existing with other much simpler levels. The distance between the leading edge and the trailing edge expands and coexistence becomes more difficult, so communication becomes very difficult.

The new paradigm is only new to us, as it has always existed within The Field as a potentiality. You create by actualizing potentialities, you discover what already exists as consciousness expands and you can handle more of Reality.

SPIRIT IS LOVE

A final word about the nature of Spirit – Spirit is LOVE. I do not mean love the emotion. I use the term Love to describe the Infinite Energy that is the manifest universe. This love is powerful and can be directed into any form or experience by the intelligence of the one expressing it. You turn this energy in to joy and into sorrow, into abundance and poverty, into closeness and distance.

I call this energy Love because it is given to us with no strings attached. We can do with it as we choose – Spirit treats us as if we know what we are doing!

When you are being your authentic self (see Chapter 17) you are coming from Love.

SPIRITUAL PRACTICE

- Sit quietly and take several deep breaths. As you inhale for each breath, imagine peace and serenity spreading throughout your being; as you exhale, imagine any anxiety or discomfort being released.

- Now, imagine yourself within your own heart. Hear the beat, feel the life force. Imagine a river of energy flowing into your heart – imagine this energy as a golden-white light. See it expand throughout your being into every cell and every particle. Imagine your entire body being lit from within, illuminated with the radiance of the golden-white light.

- Now, know that this light is Love – the energy of Spirit becoming you. See it become your body, cell by cell; see it become your thoughts, your feelings. See it become your beliefs and create them in your life experience.

- Imagine expanding this light, this Love, so that you are radiant beyond anything you have ever dreamed. See the light filling the space around you. Acknowledge that this Divine Energy does exist and that it is always with you.

- Repeat this exercise often.

PERSONAL REFLECTION

During the first months at the Science of Mind Center in Fort Lauderdale, I found a new paradox. Here, I was told that God, or Spirit, was Love, was impersonal, and was Life itself. That Spirit was Infinite – and that I could never be separate from It.

I found this a bit difficult to accept.

Over time, I did come to accept it – not because I was told to, but because I saw that when I changed my thinking toward this idea, my life changed as well. I began to see the connection between my sense of self-worth and how I experienced my life.

I was a police officer at the time. I had been in law enforcement for 17 years, seen some truly horrible things, and some truly wonderful things. I had been unable to reconcile what I had seen from my early understanding of reality. The new insights of New Thought lead me to a greater ability to see what life actually was. I began to read and study – spirituality, science, philosophy, social sciences. I discovered new authors and teachers who opened the door to a new way of seeing the world – one that worked for me.

After a couple of years of reading and taking classes at the Fort Lauderdale Center, I began to think about the ministry.

You could have knocked me over with a feather, for I had never considered the possibility since early childhood. Change often takes us by surprise, especially when we change our minds.

PART TWO

THE NATURE OF CREATION AND REALITY

"Evolution is best thought of as SPIRIT-IN-ACTION,
God-in-the-making, where Spirit unfolds itself at every stage of development,
thus manifesting more of itself, and realizing more of itself, at every unfolding.
Spirit is not some particular stage, or some favorite theology, or some specific god
or goddess, but rather the entire process of unfolding itself,
an infinite process that is completely present at every finite stage, but becomes
more available to itself with every evolutionary opening."
~ Ken Wilber, *A BRIEF HISTORY OF EVERYTHING*

"We are not human beings having a spiritual experience. We are spiritual
beings having a human experience."
~ Pierre Teilhard de Chardin

Chapter Five

UNDERSTANDING & PERSPECTIVE

"Life is mysterious."
~ Jim Lockard (probably not the only one to say this)

If you can accept that life is a mystery without simultaneously needing to have all the answers, you are in a good place on your spiritual journey. I have accepted mystery, paradox, and enigma as a part of life. The Infinite cannot be fully, logically explained by the human intellect – as frustrating as that may be to many people. In fact, very little of life can be explained in a perfectly logical fashion

"When you are analyzing, you are not looking."
~ J. Krishnamurti

"Indeed, to some extent it has always been necessary and proper for man, in his thinking, to divide things up; if we tried to deal with the whole of reality at once, we would be swamped. However when this mode of thought is applied more broadly to man's notion of himself and the whole world in which he lives, (i.e. in his world-view) then man ceases to regard the resultant divisions as merely useful or convenient and begins to see and experience himself and this world as actually constituted of separately existing fragments. What is needed is a relativistic theory, to give up altogether the notion that the world is constituted of basic objects or building blocks. Rather one has to view the world in terms of universal flux of events and processes."
~ David Bohm

I think that much of our fear and confusion in our religious traditions, as well as in other areas of life, has to do with the strong desire to KNOW that we are safe. One of the enticements of Newtonian physics was its promise that everything in its *clockwork universe paradigm* could be figured out. One of the aspects of quantum physics that makes so many want to reject it, is its promise that **nothing** can ever be figured out to an exact certainty. It is probabilities rather than certainties which seem to be the law at the quantum level of reality.

Actually, this should come as no surprise to anyone who has actually lived on this planet. In fact, the only way to believe the promise of the Newtonian view is to refuse to believe many of your own experiences, such as your experience of the inner aspects of yourself, which cannot be directly observed nor measured.

"Deep within the heart of even that which is sordid, morbid, imperfect and impure, is hidden the perfect idea, the image of eternity, the likeness of God. Society is the manifestation, through human beings, of the Eternal Presence. Somewhere, hidden in the recesses of the soul, the Eternal God sits forever enthroned. True religion is for the purpose of uncovering this God, thus revealing the Self to the self."
~ Ernest Holmes

Humans have an immense capacity for denial. I believe that Satan was created as an explanation of why everything is unpredictable. Creation myths were developed in which God was unpredictable and moody as well. In parts of the Old Testament, God became like an unpredictable uncle – someone who could not be trusted, was moody and capricious, and would allow bad things to happen to good people and vice versa. God might answer your prayers or not, apparently on a whim, and then you were told that it was not a whim at all!

Another dilemma is the seeming lack of relationship between living a moral life and having all kinds of tragedy befall one person, while another who is vile and corrupt seems to bask in comfort and great fortune. Such circumstances severely test our faith in a fair and just God, especially, given our strong desire for safety and predictability. One longs for justice and morality, when the actual nature of the universe appears to be decidedly *amoral.*

Jesus said: "Recognize what is right in front of you,
and that which is hidden from you will be revealed to you.
Nothing hidden will fail to be displayed."
~ The Gospel of Thomas, Saying 5

They asked him (Jesus): "When is the Kingdom coming?"
He replied: "It is not coming in an easily observable manner.
People will not be saying, 'Look, it's over here'
or 'Look, it's over there.' Rather, the Kingdom of the Father
is already spread out on the earth, and people are not aware of it."
~ The Gospel of Thomas, Saying 113

Every religious tradition has its version of how to deal with the confounding nature of life. Each one prescribes certain practices, forbids others, each according to its own view of reality. The most important question however is, what do *you* think?

"The further one travels, the less one knows."
~ Lao Tzu

"That is why, in all these formulations, we find an element of paradox. The
nature of Truth cannot be described by means of verbal symbols that do not
adequately correspond to it. At best it can be hinted at in terms of non sequiturs
and contradictions."
~ Aldous Huxley, THE PERENNIAL PHILOSOPHY

If paradox is an essential part of the human experience, then humans need to learn to accept it without abandoning their undeniable inner urge to be more aware of the infinite.

"A human being is protoplasm with an urge."
~ Joseph Campbell, THE POWER OF MYTH

Campbell's description is apt, as it recognizes our inner drive as the shaping element of our being. The protoplasm (body/environment) is but a vehicle for that urge. That urge, it might be said, is Spirit-as-you: *Spirit's will for you, as you.* At the same time, living a good life is, all things considered, pretty simple.

"I realize that I already know most of what's necessary to live a meaningful life – that it isn't all that complicated."
~ Robert Fulghum, ALL I REALLY NEEDED TO KNOW I LEARNED IN KINDERGARTEN

You can begin living a good life by focusing on some basic qualities: be honest, kind, loving, and as intelligent as you can. Recognize that you are connected to everyone and everything. Honor all aspects of yourself. Pay attention, listen closely, and share what you have, don't keep secrets, and whenever possible, leave things better than you found them. Learn to accept loss as part of the process, and examine who and what you are. That's a good start.

I find that while I love to analyze people, things, and situations, I only analyze what I do not know or trust. When I am in familiar surroundings, I can relax into the expectation that I am supported and nurtured. To the degree I can extend that outlook to the unfamiliar, I am a happy man. The inner urge is allowed to express and it is fulfilled on an ongoing basis. The will of Spirit will be done – Spirit's will is simply that I live a fully human life.

"I was standing on the highest mountain of them all, and round about beneath me was the whole hoop of the world. And while I stood there I saw more than I can tell and I understood more than I saw; for I was seeing in a sacred manner the shapes of all things in the spirit, and the shape of all shapes as they must live together like one being. And I saw that the sacred hoop of my people was one of many hoops that made one circle, wide as daylight and as starlight, and in the center grew one mighty flowering tree to shelter all children of one mother and one father. And I saw that it was holy...but anywhere is the center of the world."
~ Black Elk

SPIRITUAL PRACTICE

- Sit quietly with your eyes closed and take several deep breaths. Take your awareness deep within yourself.

- Think about your body and the inner intelligence that somehow operates all of your bodily organs and systems of organs. Ponder this vast array of cells, organs, glands, nerves, and fluids –knowing that all of these cells are driven by an intelligence directing what to do and when to do it. Notice your breath – it is automatic! Notice your heartbeat – it happens seemingly on its own!

- Think about how you breath air in and transform it into just what you need – how you do the same with food and liquids that you ingest – and how your body reacts to pain, injury, illness in a healing way. Contemplate this Intelligence within you.

- Now, imagine a vast, invisible Intelligence that permeates all of creation. This Intelligence permeates all energy, all form. This Intelligence has used spiritual, mental and physical laws to evolve the Universe from the Big Bang to the creation of you. Within the vastness of this Intelligence and Its Creation, can you leave room for some mystery in how it all works? Consider that your own desire and ability to consciously know cannot possibly conceive of nor understand how it all unfolds.

- Can you allow, within your own mind, for this mystery to unfold in a mysterious manner, with some guidance from your Higher Self?

- After the exercise, you might want to journal your reflections on your relationship with mystery and how it shows up in your life.

Chapter Six

RELIGION - TRANSLATION OR TRANSFORMATION?

"While it is a necessary function of translational religion to break down the teachings into understandable chunks so that they can be chewed, swallowed and digested, thereby giving coherency and meaning to our lives, we need to remain open to the transformational possibilities inherent in the insecurity, confusion, paradox, the 'beginner's mind,' the ways of not-knowing."
~ Regina Sarah Ryan, PRAYING DANGEROUSLY

P hilosopher Ken Wilbur speaks of the two functions of religion, the first being *translation*, the second *transformation*. Translation is like learning a new language; you learn to look at your life and its meaning in new ways, gaining new perspective according to whichever spirit tradition is being presented. Most of the energy of traditional religion[3] is in the realm of translation. Anytime you are dealing with dogma, commandments, right and wrong, praying for things or for healing, you are at the level of translation.

There is some confusion about these two functions and how they interrelate within various faith traditions. A very small percentage of people operate at the transformational level. They are almost completely misunderstood by people at the translational level.

Those operating at the transformational level can be called mystics; people at the translation level can be called objective literalists. There are, of course, degrees of both levels. As Ken Wilbur says, people who are at different levels do not experience the same world differently; they experience *different worlds*.

---

[3] Religion – from the Latin *religio*, which means to bind or join. Therefore, religion refers to a process.

"I believe in the fundamental truth of all great religions of the world. I believe that they are all God-given, and I believe that they were necessary for the people to whom these religions were revealed. And I believe that, if only we could all of us read the scriptures of the different faiths from the standpoint of the followers of those faiths, we should find that they were at the bottom all one and were helpful to one another."
~ Mahatmas Gandhi

The normal spiritual path goes through translation to prepare for transformation. Translation is accomplished by both society and religious faith traditions. Translation is learning how to live in the world, how to survive and thrive. You learn your culture's version of right from wrong, how to live in a family, how to live in society, how to govern your behavior, thoughts, and feelings. At each stage of your development and in each new situation that you enter, you go through a time of translation. If you learn how to do all of this with a relatively minor use of your energy, you may have enough left over to follow the transformative path. The transformative path is a dangerous and passionate one; one which requires just about all your energy. This is so because it takes an inordinate amount of energy to break free from the group consciousness of the translation level and to go within in order to connect with the interior Spirit-Self. It is literally a movement from The Field to The Void.

"A man who seeks enlightenment should seek it as a man whose hair is on fire seeks a pond."
~ Sri Ramakrishna

Translation is where you learn how to relate to yourself and to The One Spirit. Transformation is where you learn how to identify with The One Spirit. *Relating to* The One Spirit reflects a belief in dualism or separation. *Identifying with* The One Spirit reflects a consciousness of unity. The difference is all the difference in the universe. What you relate to is separate, what you identify with you become. It is a huge difference in perspective, and a critically important one in determining how you view yourself and the world.

A classic example of transformational prayer is the Prayer of St. Francis of Assisi:

"Lord, make me an instrument of Your peace.
Where there is hatred, let me sow love; where there is injury, pardon; where there is doubt, faith; where there is despair, hope; where there is sadness, joy.
O Divine Master, grant that I may not so much seek to be consoled as to console; to be understood as to understand; to be loved as to love.
For it is in giving that we receive. It is in pardoning that we are pardoned.
It is in dying that we are born to eternal life".

Through this form of transformational prayer, you seek to be used by The One Spirit for some purpose larger than your own ego desires. This level of prayer is rare – most who recite the Prayer of St. Francis do so without the intention of being used at all, but to acquire some feeling that they are good, or to *translate* lesser behavior into greater behavior. Transformation requires a degree of surrender that a *relationship* with The One Spirit cannot sustain. One must *identify* with The One Spirit, feel a part of The One Spirit, and hence worthy of that identity before being capable of surrendering to something greater than oneself.

Surrendering to a higher purpose is the essence of transformation. In a sense, translational religion is about preparing to become receptive to the idea of surrender. Most never leave the realm of translation, as most never feel one with The One Spirit, or develop the degree of self-love necessary to true transformation.

"When we pray, 'Lord make me an instrument . . .,' we are asking not only to be used, but first to be made into that instrument. It is always a dangerous prayer because it will cost us, and the self-protective mechanisms and the judgments of reason will cry out against such treatment: 'It is not fair!'"
~ Regina Sara Ryan, PRAYING DANGEROUSLY

The problem with distinguishing between translational and transformational prayer is not that there are different levels of religious focus, the problem is that so few people are aware of them, or of the inherent difficulty of communicating between the levels. The result is that today thousands read the poems of Rumi and think that they are romantic love poems to another person. Rumi wrote thousands of verses to The Beloved, to Spirit, not as romantic love poems, but as transformational expressions of Divine Love. Rumi was so transformed that he fell passionately, madly (to someone at the translational level) in love with The Beloved. While Rumi's poems may work at the level of human love, to use them as such is to misunderstand the intention of the poet.

I identify the two levels of spiritual or religious focus as **"Working with the Law"** and **"Courting the Beloved."** Working with the Law is equivalent to translation as it has to do with learning to translate concepts and symbols in such a way as to allow you to live a more effective life. What is a more effective life? That depends upon the cultural setting of the individual. For a young Muslim, it may be spending more time in prayer, for a young Christian American, it may be attaining a good and moral livelihood to support a family; for another, it may be the facilitation of a physical or emotional healing. In each case, it involves a connection with a deeper, more authentic sense of self.

Working with the law is learning to think and act in a way that brings more good. Another term for this is realization – learning to realize or attract a greater degree of good into your life through a change of psychological perspective.

Courting the Beloved, on the other hand, is the desire to identify with, to ***merge with*** Spirit and a willingness for the ego-self (even the physical self) to transform, to die. The beginning of this understanding can occur when one is in the translational phase of spiritual development; however, it is only when one has enough energy and focus to seek full realization of identity with The One

Spirit that one is ready to truly "court the Beloved." The reality is that we are *already* one with the Beloved and that our belief in separation is a false belief.

"Out there, beyond right-doing and wrong-doing, there is a field.
I will meet you there.
When the soul lies down in that grass, the world is too full to talk about.
Ideas, language - even the phrase 'each other' -
do not make any sense."
~ Rumi

It is important that you clarify these two very different approaches to religious practice so that you can be clear about them and make conscious choices about how to proceed on your own pathway.

If your goal is to be healed of an illness, or of depression, or of poverty, then working with the Law is appropriate for you. That level of focus is both appropriate and powerful in healing issues of all kinds. Likewise, if your desire is to demonstrate things (cars, houses, jewelry), people (relationships, clients, investors), or qualities (peace of mind, joy, achievement) working with the Law is the level you want. When your healing is demonstrated, or is in the process of that demonstration, you may decide to move toward courting the Beloved.

My sense of the many divergent views attributed to the teachings of Jesus is that he taught at both levels, yet the two different teachings have been viewed as one, with many people getting confused in the process. This has led to a host of difficulties for humankind (at least in the West) in the intervening 2000 years. In the Yogic tradition of India, there are six primary schools of thought for the express purpose of acknowledging these differences in approach to spirituality.

If you look at the healings attributed to Jesus in the Holy

Bible, there are some clear similarities in many of the healings depicted which reflect an approach of working with the Law. Jesus would come upon someone in need of healing, or be approached by someone. The person would indicate the problem and ask for healing (sometimes for a third party, as in the case of the Roman official seeking healing for a servant who was not present). Jesus would then do something rather strange, if you think about it. He would ask a question like, "Do you believe that you can be healed?"

He did not set up an altar, light candles, build or go to a temple, or say a prayer, or any other trapping of ritual or rite. He simply asked a question. In each instance in the Gospels, the reply was, "Yes." I assume that if anyone said no, their story was not told, which would be no surprise. Upon hearing their affirmative answer, Jesus would say something like, "Get up and walk, your belief has healed you." Then, the patient would get up, and reveal a healed condition.

If we take Jesus at his word, as reported in the Gospels in The Holy Bible, he did nothing overt to facilitate the healings. He simply made a statement (into the Law) affirming the power of the patient to realize a healing. The patient, believing that he/she would be healed, was healed. Remember the quote, *"It is not I, but my Father in Heaven, who doeth the work."*

So what happened?

Could Jesus, whom Mary Baker Eddy, founder of Christian Science called "the most scientific man who ever lived," have been very adept at using Spiritual Law? Could it have been his great clarity of mind, developed over the years of his life that very little is known about? Could his level of realization have allowed him to *know* that the desired outcome is ensured by the belief of the person involved? Did Jesus clearly understand the process of actualizing potentiality by directing the process with his mind?

"Everything that Jesus taught, every parable, every message, everything he uttered, all of his sermons — such as the Sermon on the Mount — were adaptations of different ways to show us the relationship that we have to the universal Mind, Intelligence and Law. There are no exceptions. His parables are drawn from Nature."
~ Ernest Holmes, THE BEVERLY HILLS LECTURES

And could the patient's belief actually have been the healing agent, in that his or her belief allowed a degree of receptivity to good that manifested as a healing? Could the patient have needed an outside agent such as Jesus (or today, perhaps, a medical doctor) as a means of allowing the patient to stretch that belief beyond what he could do himself?

The philosopher Voltaire described medicine this way, *"The art of medicine consists in amusing the patient while nature cures the disease."* Working with the Law includes the understanding of Law, or Divine Principle, as that which governs the flow of Divine Energy or Life into manifest form and experience. At the human level, it is subconscious belief that is the directing element for this energy. What you believe at the subconscious level becomes the law of your life, unless that belief is changed.

"As a man thinketh in his heart, so is he."
~ THE HOLY BIBLE, Proverbs 23:7

You are capable of facilitating your own healing by directing the energy of Life toward that realization (by ***thinking and feeling***), but if you don't know that, or don't believe that it is true, you don't use your belief system for that purpose. Instead, you develop systems to extend your belief so that healing can take place, albeit on a more limited basis, such as going to the doctor.

So in our model of working with the Law and courting the Beloved, many people who are advanced in the area of courting the Beloved are also known as "healers," or people who can speak the "word" and get results. They can do this because they have developed their mystical natures to a level of identifying their place in the Divine Scheme of Spirit. I believe that Jesus was one such person.

Courting the Beloved is also known as the path of the mystic. A mystic is someone who is primarily centered within, in the inner life. A mystic is a person who has mastered, or is in the process of mastering, the realization of the inner power of consciousness. The mystic basically turns away from the outer life as the main arena of action; he or she turns away from society at the level of ordinary interactions.

"The function of the orthodox community is to torture the mystic to death:
his goal."
~ Joseph Campbell

"You wear the outer garment of the law, behave as everyone else and wear the
inner garment of the mystic way. Jesus also said that when you pray, you should
go into your own room and close the door. When you go out, brush your hair.
Don't let them know. Otherwise, you'll be a kook, something phony."
~ Joseph Campbell

The turn inward in the development of the mystic begins with the transit through the 4th Chakra[4] consciousness of the opening of the heart; the dawning realization that the outer world is but a projection of the consciousness of the inner. Inside, that's where the action truly is.

"In meditating, meditate on your own divinity. The goal of life is to be a vehicle
for something higher. Keep your eye up there between the pairs of opposites
watching your PLAY in the world. Let the world be as it is and learn to rock

---

[4] See the final chapter on Spiritual Development for a description of the Chakra system. Another excellent source is *REFLECTIONS ON THE ART OF BEING: A Joseph Campbell Companion*, by Diane K. Osbon.

with the waves. Remain 'radiant,' as Joyce put it, in the filth of the world."
~ Joseph Campbell

Everyone is potentially a mystic, but I will use the term to describe those who are actually functioning in that arena of thought and action. You already are a mystic – the question is whether or not your inner mystic has been actualized in your life.

SPIRITUAL PRACTICE

- Make a list of all of the practices that you do for your spiritual development. It might include such things as prayer, meditation, conscious kindness, selfless service, tithing, and spiritual education.

- Next to each item, write whether the level of this practice in your life is translation or transformation.

- Think about the list – is there anything that you might want to change or deepen? Is it time to begin new practices, or to alter the pattern of the current ones?

- I recommend that right now, today, you add a spiritual practice to your repertoire that is transformational in nature, of course, this means that you have an honest and humble desire to surrender and trust the Universe.

Chapter Seven

FREEDOM VERSUS BONDAGE

"You arrived on this planet without an instruction manual;
and you were misinformed."
~ Rev. Dr. Charles Geddes

G reek mythology told the story of superhuman creatures with two heads which faced one another, two backs, four legs and four arms, and two sets of genitals. In some cases these were male/female, in others, male/male or female/female. These creatures were very powerful and creative.

The myth tells us that the gods on Mount Olympus became so jealous of these creatures, that Ares, the god of War, was dispatched to use his sword to cut these creatures in half. Ares did his job, and the severed halves of the original super-humans then spent their days seeking their lost other halves, thus losing their powerful levels of creativity. The gods were no longer threatened.

Another Greek myth told of the human soul having to swim through "the River of Forgetting" just prior to incarnation so that each would forget his or her true spiritual nature. This forgetting seems to be a necessary process for the psyche or soul prior to coming into human form.

Why is it necessary that we "forget" and feel incomplete? It happens to all of us, does it not? We seem to spend the first part of life becoming convinced of our own imperfection, and our adult life too often confirms our worst fears. Unless we come to realize a greater truth about ourselves – that perhaps we are complete, whole, spiritual beings, it seems that we are then destined to an existence believing that we are flawed, unworthy creatures, subject to final release only upon our physical death. We become the walking wounded, suffering through life afraid to live and afraid to die. Our own ignorance is our greatest obstacle. Spiritual awakening is the only solution. Why were we created (or did we evolve) to experience this type of life? Could it be the only way to achieve true freedom?

"To suppose that the Creative Intelligence of the Universe would create man in bondage and leave him bound would be to dishonor the Creative Power which we call God. To suppose that God could make man as an individual, without leaving him to discover himself, would be to suppose an impossibility. Individuality must be spontaneous; it can never be automatic. The seed of freedom must be planted in the innermost being of man, but like the Prodigal Son, man must make the great discovery for himself."
~ Ernest Holmes, *THE SCIENCE OF MIND*

Spiritual growth is about discovering, or more accurately, remembering, your true nature. This remembering can only come from within you. An external teacher or philosophy may serve as a guide, but no one outside of you can really know your unique truth in its entirety.

I like to think of humanity as a mosaic. When viewed from a close-in perspective, the mosaic seems to be a random collection of broken pieces of tile. However, when one assumes a larger perspective, those individual pieces form a larger image, complete and whole.

As an individual tile (personality), you cannot fully see the whole, except in remarkable circumstances. One such remarkable circumstance was the first time we saw a photograph of the earth from outer space. This was a consciousness-shifting event; it allowed us for the first time to see our planet as it appears from a larger perspective. If we had such a perspective earlier in our evolution, would we have found it so easy to create boundaries that separated us – boundaries that we defend to the death?

Another consciousness-shifting circumstance is when you

have a mystical experience, the unpredictable and powerful experience of being one with everything, called *Samadhi*. This sense of connection can come to spiritual novices and adepts alike, and it serves as a glimpse into a reality that is transcendent to one's present perspective. The descriptions of such experiences are remarkably similar – all point to a sense of unity that is so powerful and complete that it cannot be adequately described with language.

"Just as rivers flow from east and west to merge with the one sea, forgetting that they were ever separate rivers, so all beings lose their separateness when they eventually merge into pure Being."
~ Chandogya Upanishad

Humanity does not typically dwell in the transcendent. We live out our existence in the psychological/emotional/physical realm of the manifest universe. We exist in our conscious level of awareness in tune with our surroundings and our own interior space. The quality of our lives really boils down to our emotional state of being. How and what we feel is our experience of life.

So at or before birth the forgetting happens, and we strive to fit in to a world that we do not fully understand. We are conditioned to believe that our good depends on others, and that we should conform to serve society at large. One may try to do this and fail and then become "discarded" by society according to one's level of failure. Or we succeed, only to find that it does not bring lasting happiness and fulfillment. So we feel cheated, abandoned, worthless, or all three.

Still, "society" tells us that we *should* feel good as a result of our success. We *should* be happy and feel fulfilled, and if we do not, there is something wrong with *us*. We believe this, and keep playing the designated role that we have been conditioned to play – parent, worker, citizen, neighbor, etc. – never finding fulfillment or happiness. Or, we break away; "drop-out" as we used to say in the 1960's. We walk (or run) away from the corporate identity, family, or whatever constricted role is driving us insane, and take on a new life.

> *"Breaking the ideals of society is the path of the mystic."*
> ~ Joseph Campbell

Society never supports us in doing this. Joseph Campbell writes about *"climbing the ladder of success, getting to the top, and finding out it's against the wrong wall. It takes a lot of courage to climb back down that ladder and move it to another wall."*

Society wants us to conform and to support its focus at that particular moment in time, which in modern western culture means to support economic development and growth. This is the current god, the one we have decided that we cannot live without. So our worth to this society is largely about whether or not we are adding economic value or are draining it away.

Almost everything in our society is geared toward supporting the insatiable engine [5] of economic growth: our educational system, our foreign policy, even much of our spirituality is about prosperity – what other incentive is there in an economically-based culture? Even many of our charities are largely focused on getting people into economically productive roles.

To see your intrinsic value as tied up in your ability to produce economic wealth is one of the major effects of "forgetting" in our society today. Another effect of forgetting is the belief in separation, that you are not connected to me or to anyone or anything else in creation. You forget that you are part of the One

---

[5] The insatiable engine is a reflection of the human ego. The society as a whole is a reflection of the individual egos within it, and the fearful ego becomes a megalomaniac, driving this train.

Spirit, interrelated with all of creation in a dance of energy and intelligence. This is true whether you are CEO of a Fortune 100 company or a homeless person on a city street.

Your first job, therefore, is to remember your own magnificence, and your second job is to stand firm in your own greatness.

SPIRITUAL PRACTICE

- Imagine that you are shackled in heavy chains. Now see yourself breaking the chains and feel the immediate sense of freedom. Translate this feeling into a visualization of breaking the shackles of any limiting ideas or beliefs in your own life.

- Trust the power in your mind, use this technique, and watch for the results. Once you experience the change as a result of this practice, you will begin to see how the creative process operates in you and the door to true freedom will open wide.

PERSONAL REFLECTION

During my 24 years in law enforcement, I saw thousands of people living in bondage. They were trapped in a belief system that held them as prisoners and kept them from realizing the inner intelligence and spiritual freedom that was their birthright.

Some of these, of course, were those who committed crimes against other people. Some were the victims of those crimes – people who were locked into limited thoughts and beliefs, and therefore, were open and receptive to the worst possibilities of life.

Some were the police officers themselves (and I include myself), who had developed hardened shells to protect them from the horror and sadness that they encountered daily. They often burned out or turned to alcohol to numb themselves.

As I began to awaken to the possibilities within me and within others, I was able to move out of that limited thinking and even to work with others in department-sanctioned training to help develop "possibility thinking" for our officers. I left police work grateful for the experience, the friendships, and the learning that I received and enjoyed; and ready for a new expression of life.

Sometimes you have to leave the life you have so that you can have the life that is waiting for you.

Chapter Eight

CHOICE & DECISION

"The inability to make decisions indicates that you have not accepted yourself as an independent idividual."
~ *Raymond Charles Barker,* THE POWER OF DECISION

I f you are free, then you can make choices. Inner freedom exists as an aspect of your humanness, even if at the outer level your freedom seems restricted (*"Judge ye not by appearances. . ."*). In reality, you are always at choice, always free to decide what you think and what you feel. If you do not think that this is so, it is because you have made choices during your life that led you to develop and hold such a false belief. As long as you believe something that is false, you are bound by that belief. Belief is the key!

"I do not think that the Law of Mind (Spirit) in action knows us beyond our ability to know ourselves – other than as it is tied into the cosmic pattern which knows everything generically but not individually."
~ Ernest Holmes, THE BEVERLY HILLS LECTURES

My choices become limited to the degree that I come to believe in limitation. Spirit can only know me as I know myself – It does not exist as a separate personality. A rough analogy would be that Spirit knows you the way that you know an individual cell in your body. You are aware of your body as a whole – generically – but are not directly aware of the individual cells. Consistent with this analogy, science is now suggesting that one's state of mind directly impacts the cells in one's body.

Your ability to choose rests with what you come to believe about yourself, your relationship to Spirit, and your relationship to the world. If you believe in limitation, you are enslaved. Believe, or at least be willing to believe, in infinite possibilities and you are free.

You always hold the key to your own freedom.

Swami Vivekananda[6] says it so well:

"The moment I have realized God sitting in the temple of every human body, the moment I stand in reverence before every human being and see God in him -- that moment I am free from bondage, everything that binds vanishes, and I am free."
~ Swami Vivekananda

This freedom brings the ability to choose another possibility in opposition to the fear that you are separate from creation and your fellow human beings. *I believe that the fear of separation from the Creator is the greatest human fear.* The moment you acknowledge that your own beliefs are creating your subjective reality, you realize that you are co-creating your life and are no longer a victim. I say "co-creating" because your intelligence is the directing energy and the Divine Intelligence is the Life Force that you direct into form as your own experience.

"It is our own mental attitude which makes the world what it is for us. Our thoughts make things beautiful, our thoughts make things ugly. The whole world is in our own minds. Learn to see things in the proper light. First, believe in this world -- that there is meaning behind everything. Everything in the world is good, is holy and beautiful. If you see something evil, think that you do not understand it in the right light. Throw the burden on yourselves!"
~ Swami Vivekananda

Recognition of the burden is the initiation into the realization of true freedom. With freedom comes the responsibility to choose wisely and to do the work necessary to create awareness. This leads to wisdom and allows one to understand life's circumstances with clarity.

[6] From *VIVEKANANDA: Lessons In Classical Yoga*, by Dave DeLuca, Namaste Books, 2003

"Never think there is anything impossible for the soul. It is the greatest heresy to think so. If there is sin, this is the only sin – to say that you are weak, or others are weak."
~ Swami Vivekananda

If your dominant beliefs do not serve you, if they are not based on the greatest possible truth for you, you can make the choice to change them. If you are not at peace, then your beliefs are not in alignment with the greatest possible truth for you. Once you make the choice to change, you are empowered to do the mental work to transform old beliefs into new beliefs. You do this by directing your conscious mind, using intellect and emotion, to **think** a new way that is consistent with the desired beliefs.

Choice is truly the most valuable of human assets. It defines the intelligent self-awareness that is unique to human beings. When you choose from options that are not solely the automatic urges of your unconscious mind, you exercise **responsive** thought as opposed to purely **reactive** thought, which is devoid of choice. It is your ability to respond that is the essence of your power.

Your ability to choose defines you as human. Your choice to use that ability, with love and intelligence, defines you as a **realized** human being. Choice is the tool that you use to realize the fullness of life. You constantly use choice in your life; self-realized people are more aware of this power and use it more consciously.

"As we continue to unfold along the developmental path of the co-creative person the process itself leads us to **a definitive choice point***. The completion of gestation occurs when we realize that* **we will not and indeed cannot, continue to grow and develop in the confines of our egoic personalities***. A phase change occurs that is as real as the shift of an infant from womb to world. This can happen at any age."*
~ Barbara Marx Hubbard

THE POWER TO DECIDE IS YOURS

Decision is associated with choice. Decision is an active aspect of your mind. It is helpful to view decision like a simple toggle switch; it is either on or off. There is no in-between. Indecision is actually a decision, usually a decision to fail, one that generally comes about as a result of old, worn out, and self-defeating beliefs that become habitual as you go through life.

Your conscious mind contains the deciding function of your entire consciousness. Your subconscious mind is incapable of decision – it simply corresponds to conscious direction or follows its conditioned programming. Decisions are conscious processes which are sometimes made in an unconscious way – not by the subconscious mind itself, but by an unconscious use of the conscious mind.

What I mean by "an unconscious way" is that you sometimes decide without paying attention, relying on your habitual subconscious programming. Spiritual maturity requires awakened, conscious decision-making which occurs moment to moment. It requires that you become self-aware through continual self-examination which can be used as a spiritual practice. When you are awake, you have the opportunity to make decisions from your deepest consciousness, which usually springs forth from your deepest knowing, which some call your intuition. Such decisions are superior to subconsciously-driven decisions as they are imbued with greater clarity and power.

"Decision is the most important function of the individual mind. No creative process can begin until a decision is made … Having made the decision, every right idea will flow into my consciousness. Each idea will reveal itself at the instant I need it."
~ Raymond Charles Barker, THE POWER OF DECISION

Decide here and now to become decisive. Decide to use your power of choice in a powerful, positive way. In so doing, your life will change in the direction of your new decisions and the mental patterns that they create.

SPIRITUAL PRACTICE

As you go through the next 24 hours, imagine that you have a miniature version of yourself sitting on your shoulder. The role of this "observer" is to whisper in your ear to ask you the following questions:

- What are you allowing to get into your subconscious mind right now?

- What are you feeling right now?

- Is what you are about to say or do for your highest and best?

- What are you REALLY thinking right now?

Use this technique to develop an ongoing awareness of your thoughts and feelings. Also, be aware of what influences you may be letting into your subconscious mind. Take dominion by making conscious choices that are in alignment with your highest and best self – choices that are loving and intelligent.

Chapter Nine

EVOLUTION BECOMES CONSCIOUS

"This view of the nature of reality reinforces the spiritual intuition
that there is in our lives and in the world an unfolding meaning, a design,
a purpose, which is being directly expressed through each of us to the degree
that we ourselves can attune to it."
~ Barbara Marx Hubbard

Evolution versus creationism is, in truth, a false conflict. The choices are not solely between a godless Universe of random accident and a supreme being with a personality creating everything in six days. Neither side in this narrow argument honors deep and apparent (if inexplicable) truths.

If you think of God as Spirit, universal, infinite, immanent and eminent (within and without), then evolution can be seen as a natural vehicle through which creation emerges towards greater complexity. It is neither godless randomness, nor God as micromanager. Rather, it is Spirit *as* the process itself. Spirit becomes manifest through the process of evolution. Evolution is the greater emergence of Spirit through Its creation.

The Universe, then, is always evolving and so is everything within it. I am, you are, the sun in the sky is. I see evolution as intelligent change driven by an innate urge to express, directed by the individualized aspect that is changing. In other words, the intelligence is imbedded in each element in the universe, not simply "dictated from above." All of this is done through an innate tendency to use evolution as the means to greater expression.

I do not know why the Universe operates this way, or why it is self-organizing. I do not believe that the Universe was created by a Divine Personality, but I do believe that the Universe may have been **necessary** to The One Spirit to experience Itself through the only vehicle possible – the individual personality!

"If thou shouldst say, 'It is enough, I have reached perfection,' all is lost. For it is the function of perfection to make one know one's imperfection."
~ St. Augustine

Perhaps the role of duality, the essential nature of the experience of the physical universe, is to allow us to experience imperfection as a means toward growth toward perfection. The change inherent in the physical universe, where the **only** constant is constant change, exists to provide an arena for soul-development. Why Spirit would need or desire soul development I do not know, but such an explanation is at least consistent with what we experience as human beings – the need to overcome the challenges in life and to learn to live in harmony with the world around us.

We are here to grow and evolve through the deeper realization of our own nature. We grow and evolve by being in relationship to the world around us. We project Divine energy filtered through our consciousness into the world and experience that energy mirrored back to us. By this process, we create beliefs about ourselves and the world. We then spend a lifetime (or more) repeating and refining this process in order to build a self image/belief system that is in harmony with the One Truth. *"Tat Tvam Asi."* Thou Art That – You are God – Spirit AS you.

"There is an irresistible Universal and Divine urge within us to be happy, to be whole, and to express the fullness of Life. The latent Divinity within us stirs our imagination and, because of Its insistent demand, impels and compels our growth. It is back of every invention; It proclaims Itself through every creative endeavor; It has produced sages, saints, and saviors, and will, when permitted, create a new world in which war, poverty, sickness, and famine will have disappeared."
~ Ernest Holmes

"The Mind (Spirit) is no other than the Buddha, and the Buddha is no other

than sentient being. When Mind assumes the form of a sentient being,
it has suffered no decrease; when it has become a Buddha,
it has added nothing to itself."
~ Huang Po

This idea of Spirit being "infused" into the Universe shifts the debate from separation to Oneness. From such a viewpoint, physical evolution becomes a secondary aspect to the greater evolution of Spirit AS the Universe. If you think of everything being interconnected, every physical object being a surface reflection of a hidden intelligence, an intelligence that is beyond space and time and not limited in any way, then you are really ***thinking.***

Physical evolution expresses toward greater complexity, allowing for the emergence of a deeper intelligence actualizing itself in the physical realm. Evolutionary drivers push this process along, creating possibilities and opportunities for new levels of complexity and efficiency to develop. This awakening is very pronounced in humans, who are now in a position to make evolution a ***conscious*** process. This awakening is happening now, and it is experienced as a quickening, a stirring of the soul, because it is occurring in a time of accelerated change, which is an affect of evolution itself.

We are presently building to a ***crescendo*** of possibility just as living conditions become more complex, requiring a transformed human consciousness to sustain our planetary incubator. This process of creation is messy – things crash into one another, blow up, are destroyed and re-configured. Without some mess-making, there is really no creation happening.

Evolution must operate through those levels of intelligence which are the currently evolved levels of development. Up until now, what has existed is a magnificent, mysterious, yet somewhat crude process of fits and starts, with an overall pattern of growth toward greater complexity and greater and greater intelligence. We seem to be moving closer to the instantaneous manifestation of our ideas!

Thomas Troward, Ernest Holmes, Pierre Teilhard de Chardin, Barbara Marx Hubbard and others have written that self-aware humans have reached a point where we have the capability to consciously co-create the process of evolution from this point forward. If so, this is a great moment in history. The question as to whether this greatness shall be expressed in positive, loving and intelligent ways is as yet unanswered.

"In some sense man is a microcosm of the universe; therefore what man is, is a clue to the universe. We are enfolded in the universe."
~ David Bohm

When you view the events within the universe as synchronous, as driven by an enfolded "implicate order," as described by David Bohm, which has an urge to unfold into an "explicate order," then the arrival of self-awareness marks a critical milestone in the process. What had been unconsciously, or blindly driven, is now being consciously driven with the potential for intelligent foresight. This could be the end of seemingly "random" evolution, as the process is given both eyes and intelligent direction through mankind.

"Conscious Evolution signals the evolution of evolution itself from unconscious to conscious choice. It has occurred in our generation because humanity has gained the power to destroy our world, or to co-create cultures of immeasurable possibilities. It means that we are becoming conscious of our effect on evolution and must learn to guide our new powers toward a life-affirming future."
~ Barbara Marx Hubbard

"What is looming before us now is a collective jump — faster and more complex than any the world has known. We find ourselves at present in the midst of the most massive shift of perspective humankind has ever known. Clearly we are

living in a time where our very nature is in transition. The scope of change is calling forth patterns and potentials in the human brain/mind system that as far as we know was never needed before. . . . With the intersection of so many ways of being from all over the planet, the maps of the psyche and the human possibilities are undergoing an awesome change."
~ Jean Houston, JUMP TIME

So the question is not evolution vs. creationism. The question is: are we consciously evolving toward the transformed being that we must become to participate in this unfolding magnificence of what Barbara Marx Hubbard calls ***Homo Universalis***?

We are at a point in our history where we are being called to transform and transcend more certainly and rapidly than ever before. Being good enough is not going to be ***good enough***. We are called upon to excel, to transcend, to deepen and quicken our development as spiritual beings, moving beyond the inhibitions and limitations of our egoic mind and into a new level of conscious realization of Self ("I Am That). This Universal Nature is ready to be born and we are ready to act as mid-wife to birth it into full existence. The Intelligence behind it has generated both our evolution to this point, and the accelerated life conditions that confront us. <u>The time to awaken and develop mastery is now.</u>

"It is our duty - as men and women - to behave as though limits to our ability do not exist. We are co-creators of the Universe."
~ Pierre Teilhard de Chardin

The universal human is
- *connected through the heart to the whole of life*
- *attuning to the deeper design of creation*
- *experiencing a more cosmic consciousness, and*
- *desirous of expressing unique creativity for the good of the self and the whole."*

~ Barbara Marx Hubbard

The only limit to our ability to think in new ways is our self-created resistance to breaking the bondage of limited, conditioned thinking. If we can think beyond the boundaries, we can create the world anew.

SPIRITUAL PRACTICE

- Sit quietly with your eyes closed and take several deep breaths. When you become relaxed, imagine that you are floating out in the universe, among the stars and galaxies. Feel your oneness with everything that is.

- Now, imagine that the Universe begins to reverse in time and collapse rapidly. Everything moves toward a center point. It reaches a point where all of the matter and energy in the universe is collapsed into a single point, smaller than the head of a pin. Outside of this "singularity," there is nothing.

- Then, the Big Bang. From that point, everything begins to fly outward in a cosmic soup of superheated gasses. Then some solids begin to form and coalesce into larger bodies. A bit later, nascent stars form and cluster into early galaxies. You see our solar system begin to take shape, the earth coming into being as a very hot place, devoid of life.

- Things continue to progress and many changes occur on earth. Then, suddenly, there is a single cell where an instant before there was none. Then, a bit later, two cells come together, then four, and on and on. Early sea creatures form where they did not exist before. Then land creatures arise and become more and more complex. Species come and go. Dinosaurs. Mammals.

- Then a mammal comes into being who is human. Then more and more humans, culture is developed, and finally, your birth.

- Journal about what came up for you regarding evolution and your relationship to the natural processes of this Intelligent Universe. Do you sense or feel the innate urge of

Spirit to express Itself through you? Do you feel the connection to the Source of Life?

Chapter Ten

VALUE – STATIC AND DYNAMIC

*"The place to improve the world is first in one's own head and heart
and hands and then work outward from there."*
~ Robert Pirsig, LILA

Ernest Holmes, the author of THE SCIENCE OF MIND, wrote extensively about the idea of The One Spirit as Mind, or Infinite Intelligence; as Love acting according to Law or Principle. Quantum Physicist David Bohm described implicate and explicate orders – the Universe arises from the implicate order (The One Spirit) and unfolds as the explicate order (Creation). Both of these wise men see the Universe as the expression of Spirit (whatever their terms), and as unfolding or emerging in an intelligent, self-organizing manner.

Later, philosopher Robert Pirsig described static quality or value and dynamic quality or value. Static value is established value – dynamic is a new potential that is in the process of emerging, or, in Bohm's terms, unfolding. Eventually, the dynamic value emerges fully and transitions into a new static value, awaiting the next dynamic impulse to appear. Existence, therefore, is an ongoing process of emerging potential creating new expressions of reality – this is the process of evolution in all aspects of existence.

It is the way that planets form and the way that we develop socially and psychologically. When our static values are challenged, we tend to react negatively, resisting the change up to a point, then either surrendering to or eagerly adopting the new value, which then becomes static. Sometimes, we refuse to change, becoming "stuck" in ultimate dissatisfaction, because being stuck goes against our basic nature to grow and evolve.

Pirsig describes this ongoing process as one of continual

becoming. We are more acutely aware of this today as the rate of change in the world is accelerating; the world becomes more complex via this very process of emerging dynamic values. Thousands of years ago, little would change in a lifetime, or for many lifetimes. Today, the rate of change is increasingly rapid, meaning that we face a much greater degree of dynamic value than ever before. Dynamic value, because it often comes unbidden, is stressful when not understood and embraced.

Socially, our institutions hold our static values. The churches, the governments, the universities, the societies, the clubs, the corporations are all holders of static values. When dynamic values begin to emerge, they are often resisted by the holders of static values. Static values are based on tradition and history. Hence the Catholic Church resists women priests; many Americans resist same-sex marriage; General Motors resists building smaller cars; neighbors resist members of a different ethnic group moving in; corporations resist more women in the boardroom; and so on.

Personally, you have static values which create an inner resistance to dynamic values that are emerging within you. This sets up a conflict between your intellectual recognition that you need to change and a deeper feeling that you just don't want to or are afraid to. When you recognize the inherent nature of what is unfolding, you can develop a static value that supports the emergence of dynamic values – you can become open and welcoming to personal growth and change. This could be described as an element of enlightenment.

It is the same for a society, a corporation, or a church. Some corporations have a static value for dynamic change which encourages and supports innovation and change – even to the point of changing what they do to earn their profits. This is still rare, but it is an example of how we can adapt in a positive way as our understanding of the underlying dynamics grows.

Both static and dynamic values are necessary. If there is no static value, nothing holds together. If there is no dynamic value, nothing grows or develops. The tension between the two is a key aspect of the nature of our universe, which is based in duality and polarity. In the Kabala, this is described as force (dynamic) and form (static) – both are necessary for manifestation of ideas.

As you come to understand your static value patterns and recognize when a dynamic value is attempting to emerge within you, you are then able to consciously direct your own growth and put an end to sabotaging yourself. This is an important step in spiritual development for the individual, and in social development for society at large.

Of course, it is also very helpful to come to see these patterns in other people, institutions, families, societies, etc. This awareness allows you to stop blaming others for being the way they are and allows you to accept what is, letting you choose wisely when you try to influence someone or something.

YOU ARE CREATIVE

We are creative beings. Not in the sense that we create anything by ourselves – all of our energy and intelligence is from the One Spirit. You are creative – perhaps directive would be a better word – as the intelligence which directs the Energy of Spirit into your human form and experience.

The following metaphor describes the process: a person is watering a garden with a garden hose. The water in the hose represents the Energy of Spirit – always available in a consistent way. The nozzle of the hose represents your subconscious mind – which controls the shape and the flow of the energy (static). The person operating the nozzle and aiming the hose represents your conscious mind – the initiating and deciding mechanism of the process (dynamic).

The water can be shut off, turned on, made into a spray, or any variety of expressions from the hose, depending on the nozzle setting. The person watering sets the nozzle just as your conscious thoughts and feelings set your subconscious beliefs. The hose can be directed at the flowers or the weeds, again at the discretion of the person doing the watering. What gets watered will grow, just as what you feed with your thoughts and feelings grows in your experience. Or, what you "see" (in your imagination) is what you get.

The garden is like your life experience and the workings of your mind. Flowers must be planted, watered and fed, or they will wither and die. Weeds, on the other hand, just show up in every garden. Fear-based thoughts and beliefs are the weeds of your mind; loving thoughts and happy feelings are the flowers. Which do you water?

Habit can also effect the watering of the garden. Fixed, static beliefs may keep us from even allowing ourselves to think that we can have a garden full of flowers. Personal creativity is the key here – we want to learn to nurture the dynamic values within us while supporting only the positive static values. We can learn to encourage vibrant, positive change in our lives without losing all that we value, although some adjustments in our belief system will surely be necessary.

We encourage our natural creativity by deliberately changing some of our habits, from little ones like what shoe we put on first in the morning or the route we take to work, to bigger ones, like how we are in major relationships or our habitual beliefs about our relationship to money or to God.

You can begin by making it a game – do some of the little things first, then move into the more challenging habits – always seeing yourself "watering" the experiences that you truly desire by directing your conscious thoughts and feelings toward what you desire, never away from it. Take it somewhat lightly. Nurture new dynamic values and grow them into static value patterns that support your creativity, happiness and fulfillment.

Combine this with a solid practice of ongoing sacred thinking (see the next chapter) and other spiritual practices, and you change your fundamental relationship to yourself, to the Energy of Spirit, and to everyone and everything in the world of your experience.

SERVICE AS A CREATIVE, DYNAMIC FORCE

Joseph Campbell suggested "participating joyfully in the sorrows of the world." By this he meant that when one discovers their own inner radiance or God-Nature, then one sees the radiance everywhere – even in situations that others may reject or resent out of ignorance.

"Those who think – and their name is legion – that they know how the universe could have been better than it is, how it would have been had they created it, without pain, without sorrow, without time, without life, are unfit for illumination. Or those who think – as do many – 'Let me first correct society, then get around to myself' are barred from even the outer gate of the mansion of God's peace. All societies are evil, sorrowful, inequitable; and so they will always be. So if you really want to help this world, what you will have to teach is how to live in it. And that no one can do who has not himself learned how to live in the joyful sorrow and the sorrowful joy of the knowledge of life as it is."
~ Joseph Campbell, MYTHS TO LIVE BY

Here, Campbell refers to dynamic and static values – and the requirement that we come to know them as integral to the nature of the universe that we all inhabit. Saints know this – and they are able to transcend normal desire and loathing to be with the sick, the squalor of poverty, or the intellectual arrogance of bureaucracy, and still maintain their recognition that The One Spirit is present in such conditions – because It is present everywhere at all times.

When we are mired in static values, we reject dynamic values; when we have embraced dynamic values, we tend to reject static values. True transcendence requires that we embrace them both, the dynamic and the static, as well as the process of emergence and unfoldment that they represent. Dynamic value is Spirit ***emerging***. Static value is Spirit ***sustaining***.

All the great teachers have said that once you get to the point of truly loving The One Spirit and seeing yourself as fully connected to Spirit (and therefore worthy of love and good in your life), a natural desire to serve emerges.

This is not service in order to get publicity to serve one's ego; nor to receive a tax deduction. Nor is it a form of bargain and exchange. It is service from the heart based upon true compassion. Compassion can only come from a heart that is open and connected. It is the recognition that you and the other are one – without separation, within the same Spirit.

Until that level of spiritual development is reached, one gives to get, or one feels "sympathy," which is the sense of feeling separate from the other person (and relieved that you are, for that moment, at least). Sympathy is a lower level of expression; compassion is a transcendent level of expression. Choose compassion as your form of expression, as it is the highest form of human response.

SPIRITUAL PRACTICE

On a sheet of paper, list those aspects of your life that are currently in a dynamic state and then list those that are in a static state. For example, you may be in the midst of major changes in your work life (dynamic), while things in your personal life are very stable (static).

- Was there a time when they were different?

- How is the balance of static and dynamic energy in your life right now?

- Do you need to restore a sense of balance?

- Would you like to restore a sense of balance?

PART THREE

PRACTICING PRACTICAL SPIRITUALITY: STEPS TO SPIRITUALIZE YOUR LIFE

"Whether in the end, you believe spiritual practice involves stages or not, authentic spirituality does involve PRACTICE. This is not to deny that for many people beliefs are important, faith is important, religious mythology is important. It is simply to add that, as the testimony of the world's great yogis, saints, and sages has made quite clear, authentic spirituality can also involve DIRECT EXPERIENCE of a living Reality, disclosed immediately and intimately in the heart and consciousness of individuals, and fostered by diligent, sincere, prolonged spiritual practice. . . . don't just think differently, practice diligently."
~ Ken Wilber, INTEGRAL PSYCHOLOGY

"There is an almost sensual longing for communion with others who have a larger vision. The immense fulfillment of the friendships between those engaged in furthering the evolution of consciousness has a quality almost impossible to describe."
~ Pierre Teilhard de Chardin

Chapter Eleven

SACRED THINKING – AFFIRMATIVE PRAYER

"Prayer does not change God, but it changes him who prays."
~Søren Kierkegaard

Conscious human thought, as it becomes subconscious patterns of belief, is giving energy (Spiritual energy or potential) the direction it needs to determine the quality of your life experience. If you think of the energy of Spirit as a river flowing through you, then imagine your thoughts, as they form beliefs, becoming the directing mechanism by which that river of energy comes into form and experience.

Your thoughts build beliefs. These beliefs act in concert to direct Spiritual energy into form and experience – some of it becomes your physical self (by attracting materials to form your body), some becomes your emotional self, some becomes your mental self, and some becomes your experience of life. This last category is the energy that you project into the world and the world mirrors back to you as your experience.

Your thoughts are the creative points of action – the place in the creative process where you can either change direction or continue on the same pathway. Your thoughts are the gateway to all of your experience and to the creation of your mentality

"We must say that all thought is creative, according to the nature, impulse, emotion or conviction behind the thought. Thought creates a mold in the Subjective, in which the idea is accepted and poured, and sets power in motion in accordance with the thought."
~ Ernest Holmes, THE SCIENCE OF MIND

The Subjective referred to by Ernest Holmes is the One

Mind, the Mind of Spirit, of which your individualized subjective (subconscious) mind is a part. Your conscious thoughts become subjective (subconscious) beliefs and are acted upon by that medium of Mind to create your experience. This is done in concert with the thoughts and beliefs of others to create the collective experience of humanity as a whole.

If you pay attention, you will always find that a person's experience mirrors the overall tendencies of his or her thinking. If you tend toward negative thinking, you will tend toward negative experience. If you tend toward positive thinking, you will tend toward positive experience. This is cause and effect at work.

The relationship between thoughts and experience is not perfectly linear – that is, if I get a cold, it does not mean that I was thinking about getting a cold. It is, rather, holistic in that other factors do play a role in the creation of experience. These other factors are unseen tendencies and effects caused by our immersion in race consciousness, or, the thought forms of all previous and current humans. Jung called this the collective unconscious, and Ernest Holmes and others have written about its effects on individual consciousness. You might say that the "weeds" referred to in the previous chapter arise out of this race consciousness.

Race consciousness (the overall tendency of human thought) tends to be fear-based rather than empowered because it is arising out of the aggregate of all human thought up until this point in time – and it is easy to see that the majority of human thought projects fear-based vibrations. The solution to this is to consciously think loving and empowered thoughts; in doing so, you feed this higher energy into Race Consciousness and it can begin to shift (a slow process, but an inevitable one – think of dropping single droplets of clear water into a bucket of murky water. Eventually, the water will become clear).

Your overall thought patterns are the prime determinant of what you will experience, but there is a small factor that brings a level of surprise into your life. Your beliefs are subjective, or subconscious, and they operate in ways that are beneath your conscious awareness – you can never fully know your own subconscious beliefs – an important thing to remember. You can infer information about your subconscious through paying attention to your behaviors and feelings and through your dreams.

"The reason they call the unconscious the unconscious
is because it's unconscious."
~ Hans Selye

It would be an error to say that you do not direct your own experience with your own thoughts. You do. That is why it is so important to become aware of how you think and feel – thought includes feelings, too - moment by moment, and to direct those thoughts and feelings toward creating the maximum receptivity to good.

Sacred Thinking *is a type of thought discipline that holds the presence of Spirit as a constant anchor within the process of thought.* It is a thought process designed to create positive receptivity, identification with Spirit, and a clear degree of self-acceptance. It is a thought discipline that is filled with constant gratitude and acceptance. It is this thought process that leads to bliss.

Sacred Thinking can be prayer in the formal sense, but it does not have to be. Ideally, it is the way that you come to think on a regular basis. To be sure, such a way of thinking must be cultivated through awareness and disciplined practice. As one cultivates the practice of ongoing and regular Sacred Thinking, one will always have a formal prayer or treatment practice. The cultivation of awareness implies that the personality will allow a glimpse past the veil of the ego. Your consciousness does not change until this occurs – otherwise, you remain in a robotic process of habitually thinking the same thoughts arising out of the same beliefs.

*"Time set aside for prayer, or any form of remembrance or attention to prayer throughout the day, is an opportunity for the soul to feed from and grow the substance that infuses all life, and is always available. We can call it the substance of God, or divine grace, or basic goodness, or **prana**, or life force."*
~ Regina Sara Ryan, PRAYING DANGEROUSLY

If your prayers are affirmative, that is, if you recognize that you are working with a law or principle that is unchanging, rather than praying to a detached being or idea, your mental work is most powerful. In other words, Sacred Thinking is prayer that is positive and creative, with powerful intention behind it. Sacred Thinking requires that you realize your own power, your own part in the process of creation. Simply put, to think is to direct the process of creation!

The creation of your life experience does not happen without your involvement in each unfolding instant. There is no separation between you and The One Spirit, so your thought/belief process is a part of the continual flow of energy into manifestation. You are responsible for your experience because you are responsible for your thoughts. Your conscious mind is the directive mechanism that establishes the flow of energy from potential into actualized form.

When you make the choice to direct your thinking consciously, you step to the helm of the ship of your life and you take the wheel. Actually, you have always had the wheel, but you may have been living unconsciously, thinking of yourself as a victim, or perhaps believed that you were at the mercy of forces outside yourself. These mistaken beliefs have caused much misery, but ***they have never taken the wheel out of your hands!***

"Man's thought becomes the law of his life, **through the one great Law of all Life.** *There are not two subjective minds; there is but One Subjective Mind, and what we call* **our** *subjective mind* **is really the use we are making of this One Law.** *"*
~ Ernest Holmes, THE *SCIENCE OF MIND*

"We have only to believe. And the more threatening and irreducible reality appears, the more firmly and desperately we must believe. Then, little by little, we shall see the universal horror unbend, and then smile upon us, and then take us in its more than human arms."
~ Pierre Teilhard de Chardin

You think into the Mind of Spirit **from** the mind of Spirit. You cannot leave the Mind of Spirit, as there is no existence beyond It. Therefore you live, move, and have your being within this Mind. This Mind is the One Spirit, the Universal Intelligence, Atman, the All That Is, God.

Sacred Thinking is using the instrument of the imagination (your intellect combined with associated feelings/emotions) to bring you into harmony with the deepest aspects of your being. These deep aspects – called, Peace, Power, Beauty, Joy, Love, Light, and Wisdom – are the Truth of your being. When you are born, you have forgotten this, and are usually misinformed by those who raise you, since they were misinformed as well. In each generation, a few discover this Truth for themselves, or find a teacher to foster their illumination. All of us are invited to participate in this discovery.

Imagination is the key to transformation.

"It is not falling in the water that drowns a human, but staying in."
~ Anonymous

You want to become receptive to positive thinking patterns. **Refuse to remain in a negative thinking pattern.** Take dominion over your imagination. Imagine only what you desire and put the feeling of clear intention behind your thoughts. Feel the experience as though it is completed now. Become end-result oriented by creating clear expectations and developing a true sense of **knowing** that your desires are complete in the Mind of Spirit and that there is nothing to stop them from manifesting in your experience. Build a clear sense of expectation, realization, and receptivity. When you accept the Divine Nature of your being (the ability to create), your access to an Infinite Power, and your innate intelligence and self-worth, you become free to direct the energy of Spirit into any form, any experience, for yourself and for others.

This is true Sacred Thinking. Build toward it every day, every moment. You ARE the Light of Spirit in human form. Come to know and to fully accept this Truth. It is why you are here.

"The spiritual journey does not consist of arriving at a new destination where a person gains what he did not have, or becomes what he is not. It consists in the dissipation of one's own ignorance concerning oneself and life, and the gradual growth of that understanding which begins the spiritual awakening. The finding of God is a coming to one's self."
~ Aldous Huxley, THE PERENNIAL PHILOSOPHY

PRAYER-TREATMENT AS PRACTICE

An important element of Sacred Thinking is a technique called Spiritual Mind Treatment or prayer-treatment developed by Ernest Holmes. Prayer-treatment is a formal process of affirmative prayer to create a greater receptivity to good in your subconscious mind. Prayer-treatment begins with an active contemplation of the nature of The One Spirit. Use your imagination to design the highest, deepest, most powerful understanding of Spirit that you can. Make this a work in progress, an ongoing operational definition which expands and deepens as you put more energy into it (see Chapter Two, Defining God). Think often of the nature of The One Spirit.

Then, imagine yourself as a divine expression of The One Spirit. You have powers beyond measure, access to the Infinite Nature of Spirit, your immediate Creator and the ground of your being. You are worthy of good because of this. Accept your own worthiness, your own empowerment, your ability to direct your own experience any way you choose.

Next, imagine what it is that you desire – be specific and imagine it powerfully and vividly – with all your senses engaged. Imagine yourself being in only kind and loving relationship with others. What does that look like, feel like? Imagine it as though it is happening now and feel the feelings associated with your image. Keep doing this and you will embody the new vision and it will become dominant in your consciousness.

Include a step of gratitude in your Sacred Thinking – gratitude is a powerful creative energy. Gratitude is a means of expressing your perfect expectation of your good manifesting as a result of this Sacred Thinking. Then, release – turn it all over to Spirit – to Love acting as Law – and allow Spirit to coalesce about your newly created thought/feeling-form and bring it into manifestation. How does Spirit do this? No one knows, but It most certainly does do it. Test this for yourself!

The final step in sacred thinking is action – do what is in front of you *from the consciousness that you have just declared*. This means that you are mindful of what you have declared in prayer-treatment and that you maintain this mindfulness as you go about your day. When a situation arises that triggers your old reactive pattern (the one you are treating to release), you consciously override the reaction with a new response.

So the steps of prayer-treatment are:

1) **RECOGNITION** – recognizing the nature of One Spirit – Its qualities, energy, possibility. The Truth that you live in a Universe of Infinite Possibilities where nothing is every withheld from someone with a receptive consciousness. The purpose of this step is to create within you a ***Consciousness of Unconditional Love.***

2) **UNIFICATION** – recognizing and honoring your connection with One Spirit – your qualities, energy, and possibilities. The purpose of this step is to create within you a ***Consciousness of Perfect Self-Love and Acceptance.***

3) **REALIZATION** – a statement of your desire in three dimensions (words, image, and emotion). The purpose of this step is to create within you a ***Consciousness of Perfect Realization.***

4) **GRATITUDE** – a statement of thanksgiving for what is now coming into manifest form and for your realization of your connection with the Divine. The purpose of this step is to create within you a ***Consciousness of Perfect Expectation.***

5) **RELEASE** – this critical final step is the statement of trust in the Divine Law to act with intelligence in creating the demonstration of your desire. Let Go and Let God! The purpose of this step is to create within you a ***Consciousness of Perfect Trust.***

Continue to do prayer-treatment consciously and consistently until you have created a new reactive pattern – one that supports your newly declared consciousness. Recall that the old reactive pattern is a static value and the newly declared consciousness is a dynamic value, which becomes the new static value once you have it fully embodied.

There is no force outside of yourself that is going to do this for you – no godlike personality separate from you who will magically make it so. The One Spirit can only do Its work ***through*** you. The energy of Spirit is always available, always active, always corresponding to your current inner receptivity. When you change an inner receptivity from openness to sickness to an inner receptivity to health, your relationship with that Eternal Infinite energy changes. It is the ***relationship*** that is crucial – the Energy of Spirit can and does become anything that your individualized intelligence, or consciousness, directs It to become. If you see yourself as the steering power of this great energy and you decide only to aim it toward greater good, your life will become everything that you would desire.

SACRED THINKING THROUGHOUT THE DAY

You also use Sacred Thinking to get your internal house in order. I am referring to your mental and emotional houses – your state of being. What are you keeping in your house? Are you harboring grudges, anger (even rage), victim or poverty consciousness, fear, resentment? Have you repressed parts of yourself, positive and negative qualities that are inhibiting your ability to be happy in your life?

Sacred Thinking is a vehicle we can use to cleanse our inner house – to bring it to a state of clarity and transparency. If you hold grudges, learn to forgive. Forgive everyone who you believe has harmed you and then forgive yourself for holding them in judgment and for inhibiting your own joy as you did so. Give yourself some time to do this, especially if you have developed a strong belief system that justifies your anger and resentment toward whoever you believe has harmed you.

It is said that holding resentment is like taking poison and waiting for the other person to die. It does nothing to the object of your resentment, but it takes a great toll on you. If it leads to action against the other, in the form of revenge, it is even worse. There is an old Chinese proverb: "He who seeks revenge should dig two graves."

The Light within you is shining brightly right now; it always has and always will. Only by bringing the dark parts of your psyche to conscious awareness, the anger, fear, resentment, beliefs in limitation, can you remove the shadow and live in the Light. ***A great secret of life is that spiritual growth is more a process of subtraction than addition.***

SPIRITUAL PRACTICE

- Create a prayer-treatment using the five steps in this chapter: Recognition, Unification, Realization, Gratitude, and Release. Here is an example:

Spirit knows only completion, only wholeness. Spirit is perfect Love expressing perfectly. I am a part of that expression. I am the energy of Love, expressed in human form, in turn expressing according to my intelligence. Knowing this empowers me to greater expressions of joy, abundance, and health. I hereby accept perfect health as the natural state of being. I hereby remove any obstacles to that expression within me.

I am healthy, radiant, and the perfect expression of Life. I accept myself as a healthy being. All of my thinking is directed toward this belief, and my feelings are consistent with an expectancy of good health. My need for dis-ease is ended. I am now open to the natural expression of wellness that desires to express within and through me. I have perfect respiration, perfect circulation, and perfect elimination. The energy of Life flows perfectly in me at all times.

Releasing any fears, and refusing to accept any lesser idea, no matter the source of that idea, I turn to the greater possibility. I turn to Spirit within me, and I know that it is complete and perfect. I accept this Power within me, and I accept my own power to direct It for good. I am healthy and radiant, right now!

I feel the gratitude within me as I realize this Truth. I give thanks that this higher idea is now manifesting in my body and in my life. I know only the Truth! I love myself! I trust the loving process unfolding within me. And so it is . . .

- WHAT TO DO: As you read each segment, visualize the

imagery in present-tense terms. Feel the feelings which would be present if the visualization were actually happening. In doing this, you create a psychological belief that becomes active within you. This is also called affirmative prayer – the prayer is aimed at changing **your** mind, not asking God to change – you are changing in a way to bring yourself into alignment with your own inner intelligence.

Chapter Twelve

LISTENING WITHIN -- MEDITATION

"Mindfulness refers to keeping one's consciousness alive to the present reality. It is the miracle by which we master and restore ourselves."
~ Thich Nhat Hanh

When you meditate, you intentionally open to deeper aspects of your mind, inviting that deeper self to the surface, by engaging in a sacred practice which, with time, quiets the seemingly incessant surface chatter of the conscious mind. Room must be made in your mind for deeper knowing to emerge. You must become conscious of what is within you, as opposed to being ignorant of that deeper reality. So you sit quietly, focused softly on some point – your breath, a candle's flame, a mantra, the breeze in the trees – and simply allow yourself to be, taking no action but to gently bring your wandering mind back to that point of focus.

Over the months and years, this seemingly innocuous practice supports a new mental atmosphere, one that is calmer, more present, less attached, less frenetic. You are different than before.

"I have learnt silence from the talkative, toleration from the intolerant, and kindness from the unkind; yet strange, I am ungrateful to these teachers."
~ Khalil Gibran.

"Let us meditate on OM the imperishable, the beginning of prayer. For as the earth comes from the waters, plants from earth, and man from plants, so man is speech, and speech is OM. Of all speech the essence is the Rig Veda, but Sama is the essence of Rig, and of Sama the essence is OM, the Udgitha. This is the essence of essences, the highest, the eight rung, venerated above all that human beings hold holy. OM is the Self of all."
~ Chandogya Upanishad

Meditation, simply stated, is the act of listening to what is within you – that shimmering, eternal essence. The world around you cries out for your attention, but to focus solely on that which is around you is to miss the jewel of your being. As you learn to focus on the inner self, and allow that self to express more, then gradually, over time you discover a depth of being and a nature of yourself that is quite magnificent. You become stronger, less susceptible to the dramas and storms around you, more centered, balanced and connected at depth to your Inner Power.

That Power is Spirit, and It desires to express Itself through you with total clarity. It takes some courage and effort to create a channel for that clear expression to unfold, but the rewards are beyond measure. Not material rewards, although that may be a secondary effect, but more importantly a deep and profound feeling of connection – that you ***belong***.

"Whenever we moderns pause for a moment, and enter the silence, and listen very carefully, the glimmer of our deepest nature begins to shine forth, and we are introduced to the mysteries of the deep, the call of the within, the infinite radiance of a splendor that time and space forgot - we are introduced to the all-pervading Spiritual domain that the growing tip of our honored ancestors were the first to discover. And they were good enough to leave us a general map to that infinite domain, a map called the Great Nest of Being, a map of our own interiors, an archeology of our own Spirit."
~ Ken Wilber

HOW TO MEDITATE

There are many meditation practices. A simple one is to begin by sitting quietly – sitting is better than lying down, for the simple reason that you are less likely to fall asleep. Then close your eyes and think about your breathing – not to control it, just to notice it. Gently shift your attention to the point at which the breath enters and leaves your body and then hold it there.

You will drift away, and when you become aware that you

have drifted, notice what you are thinking about, and then gently return to focus on the point at which the breath enters and leaves your body. Return every time you drift away; do it gently and without judgment – it is natural to drift until one becomes used to staying in place. You want to create a sense of relaxation of the chattering "monkey mind" over time, so a sense of calm is important.

If something disturbs your meditation, let it be a part of the mediation. If the telephone rings, or a dog barks, observe your thoughts about that, observe your decision to answer the phone or not – and then, if you decide to stay in the meditation, gently return your focus to your breathing.

Do this for 20 or 30 minutes once or twice each day. You may need to apply conscious effort for a while – parts of you that are not used to being still, or are afraid of not being distracted by the outer world will become active. Most people get through this adjustment period in a few weeks.

There are many meditation practices, this one is a very basic one but very powerful. Feel free to examine others to see which one or more resonate most deeply with you. The key is to begin a practice and stay with it. One does not want to leave five minutes before the miracle happens!

There is no goal in meditation – a goal implies control, and meditation is about letting go, not controlling. You do not meditate on a problem, or set a goal, or aim to calm down or improve your health. It is a ***passive*** activity that complements other active practices, like prayer-treatment or goal setting and visualizing, which are also aspects of your spiritual practice. If you are thinking about a problem, you are contemplating, not meditating. Contemplating is a wonderful thing to do, but it is very different from meditating. Meditation does not have a goal.

"Words!
The Way is beyond language,
for in it there is
no yesterday
no tomorrow
no today."
~ Seng-Tsan (Buddhist), "Verses On The Faith Mind"

The benefits of meditation come from long-term practice. You experience subtle shifts in the physical, mental, and emotional selves. The cumulative effects of this begin to appear over time. They are side-benefits and should not be an active part of your process of meditation. The spiritual self begins to awaken – or, more accurately, you begin to awaken to your spiritual self – that is the key.

Meditation is best when you simply practice it – nothing more. It is a wonderful gift that you give to yourself, and, ultimately, to all of creation. It is a joy. Whatever form you choose, if it is a true meditative practice, and you approach it with a clear intention in a disciplined manner, you will benefit.

SPIRITUAL PRACTICE

- Begin a daily meditation practice. You can obtain a book or a video about meditation, or simply follow the basic instructions I have outlined in this chapter. The important thing is to begin and stay with it.

- You can do it, and you will not be sorry if you do.

Chapter Thirteen

THE DYNAMIC CHANGE TECHNIQUE

"The whole basis of spiritual science, of the philosophy of metaphysics and its practice, lies in the concept that the Universe is self-existent, self-energzig, self-propelling, self-knowing and self-acting, and that everything that is, takes place within one Infinite Self which is undivided and indivisible, but which out of Its own unity, creates this vast multiplication of itself, this great variation of life."
~ Ernest Holmes, THE BEVERLY HILLS LECTURES

I have mentioned visualization previously and also as part of the chapter on Sacred Thinking. Visualization, which I define as the intentional use of imagination (words, images, and emotion), is an essential element of the human creative process. Developing your ability to visualize clearly and directly is an incredibly powerful means of directing your life experience. There is an even more powerful technique, however, and I call it the **Dynamic Change Technique**. It is essentially visualization without the words or images – it is the intentional use of the emotions alone. I believe that the Dynamic Change Technique is more powerful because, essentially, when you visualize something you limit the possible outcomes and the range of what you will accept.

When you visualize a specific car, you eliminate all other cars. This is perfectly fine if you know what car you want AND you know which car is truly best for you. I believe that you need to master the technique of specific visualization before using the Dynamic Change Technique for two reasons. One, because visualizing trains your mind in a powerful way, and two, because normal visualization is sufficient for most of the changes you will want to make in your life.

That being said, the Dynamic Change Technique uses *only*

emotion. The technique itself is quite simple: imagine the ***feeling*** that would accompany the realization of any specific desire and allow the universe to "coalesce" around the energy field of that emotion. This allows a deeper intelligence to determine what manifestation would be best to bring about as a result of the feeling.

This technique requires a great deal of trust – in the Universe and in you. It also requires a willingness to accept significant change. What if the ideal manifestation of your desire involved moving away or changing careers? Are you willing to be open to large-scale change?

Our ability to visualize all potential possibilities is limited, usually to our current reality plus ten percent or so. This limitation can include personal psychological issues that keep one from expanded alternatives in any given area of life. Therefore, job-related matters are often limited to the current place of employment or the current company structure; relationship matters are likewise limited to known people or the current relationship.

"Let the imagination lay hold of it, let the feeling respond to it, let the emotion tie up with it, and let the intellect and the will give it form."
~ Ernest Holmes

I suspect that one major reason why your life-changing practices appear to not work is that the "allowed arena" of possibility is restricted to what you are willing to entertain as possible. The rest of the Universe is left out. To truly think creatively in a new way is usually quite challenging.

The Dynamic Change Technique does not have this limitation. There are, however, other concerns associated with sudden, expansive change.

For the most part, the changes we generally choose to make are the equivalent of dropping a pebble into a still pond. The ripples are small. Sudden, expansive change is different – the equivalent of dropping a large rock, or a boulder, into that pond. The ripples are large and reach to the shore – everything is affected or altered.

Most likely, the majority of the changes you wish to make are generally smaller changes that have little effect on other areas of your life. You get a new car and the expense is slightly more than before, so minor adjustments are made. You lose five pounds and your clothes are more comfortable, maybe with some minor alterations. Much of life goes on as before.

Expansive change would be doing away with your car all together, affecting many things in your life every day. Or you lose fifty pounds, requiring a different wardrobe and significant changes in the way you see yourself and interact with the world around you.

I have used the Dynamic Change Technique only a handful of times in my life. Each time, the result led to a change in my professional place of work and a move of at least 1,000 miles. One led to a number of major life changes, including where I lived, who I was married to, and what I did for a living. Oh, and the acquisition of a step-daughter and a radical change in my relationships with my own daughters.

So the Dynamic Change Technique is not for minor issues, or even normal challenges and changes. It is for when you KNOW that it is time for a significant change, and you either have no idea what form that change should take, or you strongly believe that the possible images that you can imagine do not represent the right and best solution for you.

Short of that, traditional visualization is the way to go, either alone or as part of prayer-treatment. I like to begin with the emotional feeling that I know will be present when the change I desire is in place. My process for prayer-treatment and/or visualization looks like this:

First, I begin with what I desire to change. Let's say that I want to replace my current vehicle because it needs too many repairs. The first question is – what would it FEEL like if I did not have this problem? I then imagine what it would feel like to KNOW that I already possess a car that is reliable. I play with that feeling, let it build, get comfortable with it.

Second, I ask – what IMAGE would generate this feeling within me? I might try out the image of various cars, or see myself making my monthly car payment knowing that I have gone without any repair bills. Once I have an image or two, I go to the final step.

Third, I WRITE a statement that triggers the desired image in my imagination. It might be, "I own and enjoy a brand new (make and model) automobile, which is fully reliable and under warranty."

That statement can be used alone, or more powerfully, as the third step of prayer-treatment.

The time to use the Dynamic Change Technique is when you come to realize at a very deep level that it is time for significant change in your life. The form that the change will take may be unknown. Sometimes, you have to live in the mystery (actually, you always live in the mystery, but that's another topic). But this technique is not to be used lightly, nor at a time when you are simply having difficulty picturing a minor change.

An important element of the technique is to declare that you are open to radical, extensive change. You must truly be in such a mindset for the technique to work. You should be in a place that is more than mere dissatisfaction, more than the level of discomfort that can be remedied by a specific change in your life.

I believe that we are evolving beings and that it is our nature of grow, expand, and deepen. When we make choices that do not lead to this, we know at a deep level that we are "off the beam," as Joseph Campbell would say.

When you find yourself craving something new, hearing the call from within or from without, you will likely be compelled to act. When the specific nature of the action is not clear to you, but there is clarity that something must move, the Dynamic Change Technique may be the best and most appropriate technique.

The same emotion used in the Dynamic Change Technique is also used in specific visualization – visualizing with images. The emotion is the key to change, as it gives power to the intention to create a new belief pattern. When you visualize, the most important element is the emotion that is triggered by the image.

The importance of emotion in the change process cannot be overemphasized.

"We must say that all thought is creative, according to the nature, impulse, emotion or conviction behind the thought. Thought creates a mold in the subjective in which the idea is accepted and poured and sets power in motion according to the thought. Ignorance of this excuses no one from its effects, for we are dealing with law and not whimsical theory."
~ Ernest Holmes, THE SCIENCE OF MIND

If you decide to use the Dynamic Change Technique, do your inner work first, so that you are prepared for the possibility of radical, rapid change.

SPIRITUAL PRACTICE

- If you feel that you are ready, try the Dynamic Change Technique.

- Sit quietly and breathe deeply for about five minutes. Close your eyes. Then imagine that you have your eyes closed (you have your eyes closed, imagining that you have your eyes closed) and are in a place where you know that if you open your eyes, the perfect circumstance will be present.

- Imagine knowing that the perfect circumstance will be present with great certainty, and allow the sense of positive anticipation to build until you feel that you perfectly know the feeling of having your unnamed desire. Stay with the feeling for a few moments, still imagining your eyes closed.

- Say a brief prayer of gratitude, then release the feeling and stop the exercise. Do not visualize anything – just use the emotion. You may call on this emotion any time that you think about the change in your life.

- Do this at least once each day for several days.

Chapter Fourteen

FORGIVENESS AND ACCEPTANCE

"Forgiveness is giving up all hope of a better yesterday."
~ Anonymous

 healthy psychological and spiritual life demands the ability to forgive and to accept. Forgive and accept what?

Everyone and Everything.

You must learn to forgive yourself and others for everything. The ultimate goal is to be in a continual state of forgiveness, which leads to a continual state of acceptance. This requires a different approach to forgiveness than you are likely to have learned earlier in your life. Only forgiveness can allow you to release the negative energy within that you have attached to certain memories and associations with certain people.

Forgiveness is a process that occurs within you, not outside. You forgive by releasing the energy of fear and resentment that arise when you perceive that you have been wronged in some way. Forgiveness has nothing to do with any external action – whether you ever have contact with the person you are forgiving is irrelevant. You are healing yourself by releasing the negative energy and *accepting* that whatever occurred has occurred and that you are ready to move forward.

Forgiveness is something that YOU do, not something that you ask Spirit to do. Spirit cannot forgive you, for It has never condemned you. The Holy Bible tells the powerful story of the prodigal son, whose father welcomes him home with open arms, despite the fact that he left and squandered his inheritance and lived a life of debauchery. The father welcomes him home freely because he did not condemn him – if he had condemned, he would have needed to forgive his son and himself before he could open to his son.

You may forgive someone and then make a choice not to have them in your life anymore because they cannot be trusted to be loving and supportive. In this context, forgiveness does not require any external act – it does not require that you like the person; it does require that you recognize and love the Divine Essence within them – otherwise, you retain the negative energy in your system.

As a first step in this process, you must forgive all past wounds, both those perceived as inflicted by others and all self-inflicted ones as well. I say "perceived," because a more accurate viewpoint reveals your own receptivity to everything that has happened "to you" in your life. The idea is to accept what has happened, to recognize your accountability, and to avoid placing blame. To accept "what is" without judgment is the most powerful position that any human being can assume.

"Blame is always off the track."
~ Louise Hay

Here is an exercise for you. Sit in silence with a pad of paper and pen. Go within, review your life, and gently remember incidents when you saw yourself as wounded or harmed. Beginning with your earliest memories or knowledge of events in your life, list each one on the left side of the page, with the name of the person you have blamed next to it (you can tell that you blame someone or yourself when you have strong feelings of resentment and/or anger and/or shame). Leave some space on the right side of the page for later.

Continue to go through your life and make your list – this may take several sessions. When you feel complete with this, review the list from top to bottom. Review the event and your feelings about it – then decide to forgive the person and yourself. Give yourself a few moments to "reframe" the memory to one of acceptance and forgiveness. Know that whoever was involved was doing the best they could with their level of consciousness in the moment – even if you believe that they were being malicious, they were still doing their best in the moment. People who harm others maliciously are wounded people who have forgotten how to love themselves and others. They are not strong or powerful, they are fearful and weak.

Replace any darkness with light and concentrate with a feeling of forgiveness and release. When you feel complete with this, write "FORGIVEN" on the right side of the page next to the event. Then move to the next event and repeat the forgiveness process.

When you complete the list, do a general forgiveness prayer for everything in your life until this moment for which you hold yourself or another in resentment – including any that you did not add to the list for whatever reason. Forgive yourself for every thought, word and deed for which you are not proud.

Now, resolve to live in a "continuous state of forgiveness and gratitude" in your relationship with yourself and in your relationships with everyone else. As with any meaningful change in your everyday thinking patterns, this will require significant attention on your part for a while. Gradually, you will find yourself forgiving automatically, as you learn to accept yourself as you are and, therefore, can accept others as they are.

"We must develop and maintain the capacity to forgive. He who is devoid of the power to forgive is devoid of the power to love. There is some good in the worst of us and some evil in the best of us. When we discover this, we are less prone to hate our enemies."
~ Dr. Martin Luther King

Remember that to forgive another does not require that you

be friends with them. If it is clear that they will continue a pattern of abuse toward you, or if the breach of trust is so great that it cannot be restored at this time, or if the realization is that there is no reason to stay connected to the person, you simply move on. However, when you have forgiven, you move on from a now-moment decision, not from the consciousness of an old wounding or grievance.

"Forgiveness does not change the past, but it does enlarge the future."
~ Paul Boese

"Forgiveness is not an occasional act; it is a permanent attitude."
~ Dr. Martin Luther King, Jr.

Acceptance is the capacity to acknowledge what is happening, how people are behaving, what is being said, and how you are feeling – with no resistance to what is. This is true for the past tense as well. Acceptance does not mean that you cannot make changes in any of these things, but it does mean that you do not waste energy wishing that what is, is not or that what was, was not.

"The master sees things as they are, without trying to control them.
He lets them go their own way, and resides at the center of the circle."
~ Laozi in the DAO DE JING

Accepting "what is" is a hallmark of the spiritually mature person. The denial of what is leads to suffering – every time. Accepting what is makes space for freedom.

"You move totally away from reality when you believe that there is
a legitimate reason to suffer."
~ Byron Katie, LOVING WHAT IS

*"What is **is**. You don't get a vote. Haven't you noticed?"*
~ Byron Katie, LOVING WHAT IS

When you come from a place of acceptance, you are empowered because you are not wasting time and energy resisting what already is. Buddhists call this "non-attachment" or an affirmative consciousness where you refuse to allow outer events to dictate your inner reality. Such a state of consciousness requires significant practice, including prayer, meditation, and the observance and direction of thoughts and feelings throughout the day (Sacred Thinking, Chapter Eleven).

When you can accept what is, you also have the ability to maintain a state of calm and effectiveness. You will be offended much less often, or not at all. (Imagine that!) You will not be drawn into the false drama of those who cannot accept what is. Such a state of acceptance is very positive and very powerful.

High-functioning relationships based on the recognition of Spirit within always have the element of forgiveness as an active dynamic of the relationship. In fact, a continual state of forgiveness is essential to the ability to be fully present and open to yourself and the other person in relationship. When one does not forgive on a continual basis, the relationship suffers, whether from the state of being watchful for the other to do something that disappoints, or from the state of being in resentment of some prior act or omission (or the perception of an act or omission).

Only through continual forgiveness can you be fully present in the relationship – present in the moment to enjoy the relationship. The ongoing recognition is that the other is to be loved and honored even in his or her imperfections, and the same goes for you. True honesty is essential for a high-functioning relationship, and true honesty can only be present when you are fully open to yourself and the other.

"Nonattachment is the most realistic of attitudes. It is freedom from wishful thinking, from always wanting things to be otherwise."
~ Marilyn Ferguson, THE AQUARIAN CONSPIRACY

As you move toward the mastery of the ongoing consciousness of forgiveness, acceptance, and gratitude, you will find old feelings occasionally coming to the surface. This does not mean that your work has been insufficient – these are simply the remnant of the feelings about the old issue. Simply accept that this is so and allow the feelings to drift away. Then forgive yourself again. Denial or resistance merely prolongs the release of the old issue and, therefore, prolongs suffering.

"The weak cannot forgive. Forgiveness is the attribute of the strong."
~ Mahatma Gandhi

SPIRITUAL PRACTICE

- On a piece of paper, make a list of the people who you feel you would like to forgive. Begin with your own name.

- Review each name (do your own last). Think about the perceived offense, feel the feeling associated with it. Now decide to remove the negative energy from your system by releasing your idea of the person to their own path. Bless yourself and the other person. Take as much time with each person as you need. Then go onto the next.

- Once you have finished the list, resolve to live in a state of *continuous forgiveness* from now on so that you do not have to make any more lists. Mark your calendar to check your progress once a week for four weeks, then monthly.

PERSONAL REFLECTION

On Easter Sunday, 2008, I received a telephone call just after midnight. It was my daughter, Heather, who was visiting her mom and her sister, Caitlyn in Fort Lauderdale. I was in California, where I was living with my second wife, Dorianne, who had just left that morning for a week in our condo in Big Sky, Montana, where she was going to write and study in the solitude of that beautiful place.

It was just before 10:00 pm, the day before Easter in California, just before 1:00 am on Easter Sunday in Florida.

"Dad," Heather said in a shaky voice . . .

Caitlyn, who was 18 and due to graduate from high school in about 8 weeks, had been out to dinner with her mom, Heather, and Caitlyn's boyfriend. It was their six month anniversary of going together. After dinner, Caitlyn, her boyfriend, and two other friends went to the movies. On the way home, in a driving rainstorm on I-95, he lost control of his pickup truck and went off the road. Caitlyn was ejected and the truck rolled over her. She died at the scene. The other three walked away from the accident. Caitlyn was not wearing a seat belt.

Modern communications being what they are, my ex-wife had been called before the paramedics arrived. I was called as they were working the crash. She was pronounced dead at the scene.

All I knew from the initial call was that there had been an accident and that they did not think she would survive. The other information came in through the next several hours. Between calls, I cried, cursed, collapsed. I called Dorianne, but the phone was unplugged at the condo. I called my prayer-partner, Candice, and we prayed for a while. My mind raced – wanting to deny, wanting to blame, wanting to hold myself responsible (Caitlyn had been troubled by my recent divorce and re-marriage), wanting to do SOMETHING, but being 3000 miles away in the middle of the night.

I called Delta Airlines around 2:00 am. The operator, when hearing why I was calling, put me on hold for about 15 minutes. When she came back, she told me how upset she was when I told her. She said, "Sir, we will get to where you need to go." I exchanged the tickets I had bought to attend Caitlyn's graduation, scheduled for eight weeks later, for a flight to Fort Lauderdale the next morning from LAX, with an open return. The Delta agent assured me that Dorianne and Grace (my step-daughter with Dorianne) would be taken care of as well. All fees were waived.

By 3:00 a.m. or so, the calls from Heather stopped for the night. I tried to understand what was happening – how it could be happening. I went through all that I knew from every source of learning I had been exposed to. I remembered a line from one of my New Thought teachers. He said: "Reality divided by logic, always leaves a remainder." I realized I would never know why.

I packed a bag for the morning, and then I prayed, meditated, and waited. As morning came, I called my co-Pastor and told her that I would not be there for the Easter service. We prayed together as well. Then I called a good friend from my Center in Westlake Village, and asked for a ride to LAX. I called Florida for an update – nothing really new. I called Dorianne in Montana, this time getting through. We cried and prayed. Caitlyn had come to live with us for five months in 2007, so Dorianne was devastated by the loss. At about 8:00 am, I left for the airport.

The next three weeks were spent in Fort Lauderdale. I was overcome by how much love and support came forth. Over 600 people came to the memorial service at the Center for Spiritual Living, Fort Lauderdale. People came from all over the U.S. Another service was held at her Catholic high school for the entire student body upon their return from Easter vacation. The time went by in a blur; we did what needed to be done. After a while, we went back to California.

I cannot imagine trying to get through such an experience without a solid spiritual practice, and without a well-developed ability to accept what is and to forgive myself and others.

There were so many possible ways to place blame or feel victimized in this case! There was her boyfriend who should have been a better driver and should have made sure she wore a seat belt; there was Caitlyn herself, who constantly had to be reminded to wear a seat belt, and who had been in five accidents since getting her license, one in which she suffered a severely fractured leg; there was me, who left the family and helped to create a sense of dislocation and sadness in Caitlyn; and there was God, or fate, or destiny, who took her when she wasn't even driving, with no alcohol or drugs involved. There was plenty to blame, if I wanted to blame.

I think I discovered and affirmed several things in dealing with Caitlyn's death.

- I discovered that grief does have a bottom. The years of prayer-treatment, meditation, and spiritual contemplation had provided me with a sound foundation that formed a "bottom" to my grief. I could grieve openly and powerfully, never fearing that I would fall into a pit of despair.

- I affirmed the value of having spiritually-mature people in my life. Throughout the experience, I had the unwavering support of a variety of people, some ministers, some family, many friends and acquaintances, who understood and supported me and my family completely.

- I discovered that I could grieve and recover from that grief. I will always feel the loss of Caitlyn, but I know that I have healed the deeper wounds from this experience.

- I discovered that learning to live in the mystery is the only way to move though life with any true sense of happiness and fulfillment. The "remainder" is huge in every life.

- I affirmed that Caitlyn was, in her human experience, a good person. The people who came forward and said that they were touched by her love, her wisdom, and her refusal to let anyone fail to be aware that they could do better, were very powerful. She contributed to worthy causes, and touched hundreds of lives in her short time here.

- I affirmed the value of forgiveness and acceptance. I accept that she is dead. I forgive myself and everyone else. Caitlyn, too.

Chapter Fifteen

SERVICE AS SPIRITUAL PRACTICE

"I don't know what your destiny will be, but one thing I know: The ones among you who will be really happy are those who have sought and found how to serve."
~ Albert Schweitzer

The ultimate goal of spiritual practice is to realize your oneness with The One Spirit – to train your mind to that level of realization. As one pursues that goal, one passes through a wonderful step in development which includes the quickening of a strong desire to serve creation. This step in awakening is recognized in every great faith tradition and is woven into the social fabric of every human culture and community. Remember, the word "religion" comes from the Latin *Re* and *ligare*, meaning to re-connect.

"The sole meaning of life is to serve humanity."
~ Leo Tolstoy

"Only a life lived for others is a life worthwhile."
~ Albert Einstein

"Kindness in words creates confidence.
Kindness in thinking creates profundity.
Kindness in giving creates love."
~ Lao-Tse

A COURSE IN MIRACLES says that when service is selfless – that is, when it is freely given out of love with no thought of return or reward – it is a spiritual practice. When we give freely, we represent the highest Spirit Nature within, the truest form of human love. When you practice service, you open to the transcendent in a new and powerful way.

There are ample opportunities to serve humanity every moment of every day. When you begin to notice them, your heart fills with gratitude. Service can be for an organization or a cause, but it can also be a kind word, a prayer, the gift of listening, telling someone the truth about them (such as the fact that they are magnificent beyond measure), or any expression of unconditional love and connection that comes spontaneously from the heart. It makes no difference if one or a million are served. It is the unconditional nature of the act that is sacred.

What if you do not feel an unconditional loving urge to serve? Begin by acting as if – find a cause, a person, something that is good and true – and serve through conscious effort. After a time, if you are true to it and to yourself, a shift will happen and the service will become selfless. That is the gift of service, and it is priceless. Remember that selfless service does not mean that you are not rewarded by the service – nothing is more fulfilling in life than to give meaningful service out of love to another – just ask any loving parent.

There are countless ways to serve others. They range from living a life of service to volunteering for some organization or cause that is meaningful to you, to taking a moment to really listen to someone. A good place to begin is in an area where you feel lack or limitation. If you are having health issues – serve at a hospital or hospice; financial issues – serve at a homeless shelter or in a program for the poor; relationship issues – volunteer at a shelter for battered spouses or children.

When you give in the area in which you suffer, you create a healing process for yourself while you serve others. When you do this, you often find yourself staying in service even after your own issues are healed. That is the wonder of loving service – it is a benefit to all and to humanity as well. A good friend of mine, after years of participating in Alcoholics Anonymous, remains in AA because he loves the opportunity to serve as a sponsor to those new to the program. His addiction led him to a life of service.

We all seek meaning in life. A life without service is a life without meaning.

"The most beautiful things in the universe are the starry heavens above us and the feeling of duty within us."
~ Native American Proverb

So we have covered these practices – Sacred Thinking or Affirmative Prayer, Meditation, Forgiveness, Acceptance, and Service. To these you can add spiritual education, tithing, kindness, and myriad others, all essential in one way or another to the cultivation of awareness and the opening of the heart. Now, we will explore spiritual development, and then close with the element of finding your Authentic Self.

SPIRITUAL PRACTICE

- On a sheet of paper, make a list of ways that you can serve others. The list can include anything from volunteering for organizations to saying a quiet prayer for your neighbor.

- Find the one thing that "makes your heart sing."

- Go and do it.

Chapter Sixteen

SPIRITUAL DEVELOPMENT
Unfolding of the Self

"The spiritual evolution obeys the logic of a successive unfolding; it can take a new decisive main step only when the previous main step has been sufficiently conquered: even if certain minor stages can be swallowed up or leaped over by a rapid and brusque ascension, the consciousness has to turn back to assure itself that the ground passed over is securely annexed to the new condition; a greater or concentrated speed (of development, which is indeed possible) does not eliminate the steps themselves or the necessity of their successive surmounting."
~ Sri Aurobindo

When you look at human spiritual growth as a developmental process, one occurring in specific and discreet stages, it brings a deeper awareness to the process. There is, to be sure, a somewhat confusing array of models out there. The work of Ken Wilber is helpful in comparing these models, and Wilber's own, four-quadrant model (AQAL) is a very powerful and useful developmental model. Another example of a developmental model that is clear is the 12 Steps of the addiction recovery movement.

Simply put, the developmental idea says that humans go through a number of stages from pre-infancy through transpersonal levels of consciousness. The lines of development include physical, mental, emotional, and spiritual, each with its own stages. Early stages of development occur relatively automatically, although the ways that we interact with our world have a lot to do with how we develop within stages and how we develop to higher stages.

We are learning more about adult development as well, giving insight into the stages, understanding what tends to happen in each, and creating models of higher states for seekers to use as guidelines. Newer models such as Spiral Dynamics (Beck & Cowan,

1995), and the work of Carol Gilligan, along with the synthesizing work of Ken Wilber, offer great promise for exploring more advanced levels of human potential.

The value of developmental models is twofold. First, since the models are universal, you can get a sense of where you are at any given point in development and whether your particular manifestation of the stage is healthy or pathological. This allows you to adjust toward a healthy version of that stage of development. Second, many models offer a description of higher levels of development, allowing you to seek to bring yourself toward specific developmental goals, using certain methodologies (such as spiritual practices, education, therapy, etc.).

The tendency is to have an innate urge toward greater expression of your inner potentials. You desire to actualize these potentials in an ever-deepening and expanding sense, moving toward greater self-realization and expression. *Life feels better when you are following this urge.* Through spiritual practice, these potentials become conscious. Understanding the developmental nature of human growth can be a great help in allowing you to consciously direct your spiritual growth.

Many great spiritual traditions recognize that as human beings, we seem to be designed to unfold, to develop, toward deeper awareness. Even when this does not happen, the urge to do so is present. It may present itself as an empty feeling in early or late adulthood, when you sense that something that was supposed to happen did not happen. It may present itself as a strong desire to follow a spiritual pathway or to learn philosophy, or to make a major change in the way you use energy in your life. *Spiritual development can be described as being driven by an inner urge of Divine Intelligence to express combined with a conscious willingness to have this happen.*

"Human beings are protoplasm with an urge."
~ *Joseph Campbell*

"Spirit slumbers in nature, awakens in mind, and finally recognizes itself as Spirit in the transpersonal domains."
~ Ken Wilber

The stages of development can be illustrated as any number of categories. I will use as an example of a model with three major categories, each consisting of sub-categories. If you are familiar with the Seven Chakras as a model, my first category would relate to Chakras 1 to 3, the second category to Chakra 4, and the third category to Chakras 5 to 7.

The first category has to do with the development necessary to live in the physical world – survival, sexuality and creativity, and power issues exist here. This is where you learn to live in the world, to survive, to create a family, a career, a fortune; to engage in politics, business, sports and relationship. Religion at this level primarily deals with right and wrong and institutional authority as the primary structure. One's world view here is one of fear, and the placement of power is outside one's self. Things happen "to" you at this level.

The second category, symbolized by Chakra 4, the Heart Chakra, is that of spiritual awakening, or the dawning realization that there is more to life than meets the eye. This awakening is an inner process, and is not necessarily associated with being "religious" as in the first category. The awakening here is a genuine, inner-directed process of spiritual realization that can be supported or hindered by traditional religious affiliation, depending upon the level of approach of the tradition.

This awakening level of development is extensive, and the completion of this level includes a transformation of the basic motivational energies of the person. You move from an egotistical, fear-based motivation toward a true sense of self-empowerment, where fear is no longer the defining quality of energy. At the completion of this level of development, things happen "through" you. Barbara Marx Hubbard described this shift as "from Ego to Essence." At this point in human development, very few people develop to an extent that takes them all the way through this level. Most of those that enter this level get stuck, or fall back into the first level. Any time you get stuck or fall back, life tends to become very frustrating for you.

The third category, symbolized by Chakras 5 to 7, represents what we will call higher spiritual development. At this stage in human evolution, very few people reach this as their primary level – very few. Here, the energy within is spiritualizing your thoughts, feelings and actions. One still goes to work, drives in traffic, and has relationships, but they are approached from a very different perspective, one of defining and expressing one's relationship with The One Spirit. The Buddhist saying, "Before enlightenment, chop wood, carry water. After enlightenment, chop wood, carry water," applies here.

At the upper levels of the third category, one is in direct relationship with Spirit most of the time. This is a mystical way of being, that is, one spends most of one's thought/feeling time aware of what is occurring within rather than without. One comes to view the external world as a projection of one's own internal world; you see yourself as co-creative with Spirit. This is a blissful state, because at this level, one has attained a deep realization of one's own God-Nature, one's own goodness and power. At this level, things happen "as" you.

These categories are universal, they apply to humanity generally, and the differences between people within each category or level are primarily cultural. There are other factors which affect the way one experiences each category. For example, seeking category three awareness is more common in India than in the

West. Learning about your own development through these stages is essential to solid spiritual growth.

All individuals exist at all of the levels of development in terms of their inner potential. You will have a "center of gravity" where you happen to be in terms of actualized development at every point in your life. As long as there is some progress going forward, your life will feel "right" more often than not. When your life does not feel "right," it may well be that you are somehow blocking yourself from moving to a new level of development.

SPIRITUAL PRACTICE

- Contemplate your own level of spiritual development. You might begin by making a list of spiritual aspects and practices, and giving yourself a grade of 1 to 10 in each area. If you have a 2 in service, that is an area to focus on. If you have a 10 in meditation, bless yourself and continue your practice in that area.[7]

- Given the entire list, can you see ways to increase your spiritual development by making changes in the scores on your list?

- Then go ahead.

---

[7] See *REFLECTIONS ON THE ART OF LIVING – A JOSEPH CAMPBELL COMPANION*, by Diane K. Osbon for a wonderful description of the Chakra system and related spiritual development.

Chapter Seventeen

LIVING AS YOUR AUTHENTIC SELF

"Follow your bliss."
~ Joseph Campbell

Your bliss, according to Joseph Campbell, is your deepest, truest identity. It may be called the Christ Consciousness, Buddha-Nature, God-Nature, Higher Self, Self, Authentic Self, and many other names. Bliss is the state of being aware of that true identity with clarity and certainty. It is a state of being awake, just as being in ordinary daily routine consciousness is a state of being asleep.

When you awaken to your true nature, you have found the jewel of life. But Campbell in his wisdom, does not merely say *find* your bliss. He says *follow* your bliss, which means to live your life from that centered space, releasing any of your old ways, beliefs, attitudes and habits which are inconsistent with that deeper identity. It is a state of true transformation, perfect 4th Chakra awareness, which must be followed by action. This action is refined in 5th Chakra awareness and then rewarded in 6th Chakra existence (this would be the second tier of consciousness, or value system complexity in Spiral Dynamics™ - Graves, Cowan & Beck).[8]

The developmental pathway briefly described here is innate in you – you are designed to unfold into greater expressions of beingness in this "school of life." This process of unfolding spiritual

---

[8] In spiritual development, the first three Chakras represent "living in the world" – survival, sex and creativity, and power. The 4th Chakra represents the stage of awakening to Spirit at great depth. Chakra 5 is the discipline of spiritualizing the lower centers and appetites to bring them into harmony with the new Spiritual identity as realized. Chakra 6 is the direct experience of Spirit – a place of bliss and the highest place one can attain and still be in form. Chakra 7 is Buddha Consciousness, where one is no longer in form.

development is a part of all aspects of your nature – physical, emotional, mental, and spiritual. It is a natural part of being human, from the point of the joining of sperm and egg (actually well before that in your spiritual nature), through the final breath of your physical body. All of these aspects are of the same nature. Then your Spirit Nature continues on, perhaps in other incarnations, perhaps not. I'm not sure.

What I am sure about is that you were born with an innate drive or urge to express as a Divine being. Nothing short of infinity would ultimately satisfy you. This urge continues to drive you forward, even if you have experienced great despair or great success in your life. Remember, you are, in effect, protoplasm with an urge, according to Joseph Campbell. ***That urge is dynamic value. Your Spirit Identity and what it seeks is the greatest expression of the individualized aspect of The One Spirit that is within you.*** It urges you to demonstrate your magnificence, to stand in your own greatness.

> *"To thine own self be true, and it must follow, as the night the day, thou canst not then be false to any man."*
> ~ William Shakespeare, *"Hamlet"*

Shakespeare's famous quotation is an accurate statement about your nature. When you do the spiritual and mental work to find your center, and put the energy into the process of living authentically from that center, then you cannot be "false to any man." You cannot be untrue any more. You become transparent, meaning that you are the same in any company, completely, authentically yourself. You identify with and express your deepest self without concern about pleasing others or fear of being rejected. ***When you have accessed your own depths and the spiritual strength within, you fear nothing.***

"Dare to declare who you are. It is not far from the shores of silence to the

boundaries of speech. The path is not long, but the way is deep. You must not only walk there, you must be prepared to leap."
~ Hildegard Von Bingen

Hildegard, from the Christian mystical tradition, brings forth the necessity of risk-taking as a part of the spiritual pathway. Dynamic value is seldom welcomed by static value. Your static beliefs and ego-needs and other people and institutions will try to get you to stop seeking your Truth, to stay with the status-quo, to fit in at all costs. Turning away from this voice takes courage. You have courage. The fact that one must express courage acknowledges that there is fear present. If you have no fear, you need no courage. So you have fear – wonderful! If you have fear, you have courage. Decide to be courageous today.

"Seek out that particular mental attribute which makes you feel most deeply and vitally alive, along with which comes the inner voice which says, 'This is the real me,' and when you have found that attitude, follow it."
~ William James

A great gift of the New Thought wisdom traditions is the awareness of our Divine Nature – our access to an inner power that is part of a Universal Power. While many have lost their way and made this Power seem small and even petty, the Power Itself has remained unchanged. If you have turned from this Power, or have simply avoided it (except perhaps for an inner voice that has haunted you from time to time), that Power AS YOU is still fully present, fully available, awaiting your recognition of it. As Ernest Holmes wrote, ***"the Power can only do FOR you what It can do THROUGH you."*** Your receptivity to your good, to the Universal Good is the key. This Power is completely available to you – and you can most completely access It by living as your Authentic Self – by following YOUR bliss.

STEPS TO FOLLOW YOUR BLISS

- You begin with an awareness of Spirit. God in Everything – Everything in God.

- You move to the awareness that you are one with Spirit – that there is no separation.

- Then you take dominion over your thoughts and feelings and use your imagination to create new beliefs based on positive expectations of love and good in your life – you come to know, and know **absolutely**, that you direct your subconscious mind with your thoughts and feelings and you take full dominion over the creative process as you.

- You direct your thoughts and feelings clearly, intelligently, and lovingly to create beliefs that support you and your good in your subconscious mind.

- Then you **know** and act as if these are true until they manifest.

- You meditate, listening to the voice of the Universe as the deepest part of yourself.

- These practices heal. Healing is simply a return to Truth. Illnesses, sadness and limitation can only exist when you believe something that is not ultimately True. **Facts change, Truth is unchanging.** What are you focusing on?

- Psychological and spiritual growth are most often by way of challenge, sometimes with suffering. No matter how significant the challenge, how great the suffering, there is always the opportunity to grow from the experience.

- You serve and give and forgive and accept and take some risks and enjoy yourself and other people and honor all of creation – ***and*** you experience loss and sadness, and challenges, too, and the grief that goes with them – and you live in bliss on this wonderful journey of your human lifetime.

- After doing this for a while, you develop a consciousness of intelligence, love and connection, and it becomes automatic – just being who you really are, with ease and grace. There will always be aspects of life that are difficult. When you make the transition from ego to essence, you come to know more fully that your experience of reality is based upon your own consciousness, not on the facts of the outer world as they show up.

- The natural effects of such a personal transformation are ***kindness and compassion.*** Kindness is the expression of love. It is neither some forced politeness nor cultural habit, nor a manipulative expression, but an authentic expression of the realization that you ***are*** love and so is whomever you are addressing or speaking about. When you are automatically kind, without the need to repress anger or irritation and to project being nice, when it is truly reactive and natural, you are in a state of being that is blessed. You are blessed. Compassion is acting from a deep, basic awareness that you are one with everyone and everything else – compassion is the expression of Spirit by means of you.

- Follow your Bliss – find the Spirit in you and live from that Center. Step into the Light in which you have resided since before the Big Bang – the timeless, eternal Void out of which arises all of Creation.

"You are my beloved Son; with you I am well pleased."
~ THE HOLY BIBLE, Mark, 1:11

As I wrote in the Introduction: You are a child of the Father – of the Father/Mother God, the One Spirit. You contain the Christ Consciousness, the Buddha Consciousness, the Light of the Spirit, within you. And the Creator, however you view this Power, *is* well pleased with you, loving you unconditionally by providing you with all that you need to live a happy and fulfilling life – requiring only that you use your intelligence to accept your good, not to turn away from it. The One Spirit is the Action of Life, the Animating Force within you and everything that exists. Take joy in this. Let your mind entertain it and see how it feels to you. Listen to the wisdom of your heart. Choose to open to the Transcendent. It is there, waiting patiently – for YOU.

SPIRITUAL PRACTICE

- Meditate deeply on the Authentic You. What are you really like at the deepest level of your being? What are your highest values?

- As you go through your day, monitor your behaviors – are you living from your inner values? Have you "sold-out" to what others want or expect of you?

- Make a list of what you would be doing in your life if you had made all of the big decisions along the way from your deepest inner values. How different would your life be today?

- What changes are you willing to make as a result of this practice?

CLOSING THOUGHTS
FOR A NEW BEGINNING

I wrote this book to present my view of the nature of The One Spirit, and how spiritual practices, including Sacred Thinking, can bring you to a deep realization of your connection with Spirit. This view comes from over 20 years of studying, teaching, and living spiritual principles to the best of my ability. I hope that you will connect to Spirit by means of the ideas I have offered. I am on my own pathway toward the realization of who I am, and my teachers have been many, some of them are quoted or referenced here. I trust that others will appear as I proceed on my pathway, just as they always have when I needed them. I do not believe that a personal idea of God and of self can be static. You and I are part of something infinite, something in constant motion, constant vibration, something beyond our comprehension, and yet it is something that is within our hearts in a way that I could never describe fully.

I also believe that the only good theology (Divine logic) is one that leads to happiness and fulfillment in this lifetime, not in some promised afterlife. I believe that we have learned enough through suffering and are now ready to make joy our default setting. I also believe that you and I are being called by the Universe to awaken to our True Nature with greater urgency than ever before. We are truly at a turning point in human evolution – we need to rise to a greater potential quickly or we risk falling back into chaos and even extinction. We have some cleaning up to do – cleaning up of the human psyche, what Jung called the Collective Unconscious and Ernest Holmes called Race Consciousness – before we are ready to move forward without the weight of our collective false beliefs and the fear that accompanies them.

But that cleaning up need not be arduous. It can be a joy when undertaken from a consciousness of positive expectancy nurtured by a firm belief that you and I live in a supportive

Universe – one that always provides exactly what we need when we need it. If only we can develop the level of receptivity necessary to accept the boundless gifts bestowed.

"Behold, the Kingdom of the Father is already spread out upon the earth and people are not aware of it."
– Jesus in the Gospel of Thomas, saying 113

In the Great Scheme of Things, it would be fine if human beings were to become the next species to become extinct. The Universe would keep being the Universe, The One Spirit would keep expressing through Creation, and the great and lesser celestial bodies would keep spinning and speeding apart. But the potential future generations of human beings would be denied their part in that great orchestration. That would be a great frustration of potential – for I believe that we humans have a great deal more to bring to the Universe. Our legacy to the cosmos should not end by fizzling out. And saddest of all (from our perspective at least), the Universe would lose a self-aware aspect of creation which was on the verge of mastery.

The door is open to another possibility – to the greater expression of love and energy arising from a newly awakened humanity imbued with an emerging intelligence that is pure Love. We are literally standing on the verge of our transformation into transcendent beings. If only we will choose to wake up.

I am optimistic that we will awaken in time. Do you care to join me?

SPIRITUAL PRACTICE

- Go back and review all of the spiritual practices in this book and what you did with them.

- Create a set of practices that you can commit to on an ongoing basis and begin.

- Practice them regularly, with clear intention and purpose.

- Love yourself more every day.

- Use Sacred Thinking to uplift your self-concept and grow closer to Spirit.

- Engage Life.

- Be open to Love and Joy.

- Come to know Spirit by knowing yourself.

I love you.

PERSONAL REFLECTION

I am a work in progress. In my ministry I try to make this clear to everyone who comes to me. You cannot live from my truth, and I cannot give you your truth, but I may be able to point you in the right direction so that you can find your truth for yourself.

Ministry is, for me, an ongoing gift. It allows me to teach, to support and nurture others, and it gives me constant feedback on my own shortcomings. To the degree that I have realized my own authenticity, it has come via two areas of my life: through ministry, and through family. I have been blessed with wonderful people in every version of family that I have experienced. All of us are flawed, but many of us rise above those flaws to loving expression – more often than not we do that BECAUSE of those flaws.

Imperfection is the essence of human existence. We are all perfectly imperfect. It is that very imperfection that allows us to grow in wisdom, in the capacity to express love, in the ability to make decisions from an empowered sense of self. Imperfection also allows us to understand when we fall short, or have a setback.

As I go forward from this point, whatever form my life may take, I will grow in all of the positive qualities that I can cultivate. I will release all that no longer serves me in that growth. I will have creative, loving, intimate relationships; do work that is of service and that is challenging and rewarding to me. Above all, I will seek a deeper relationship with the One Spirit through Sacred Thinking. And I will find it – continually.

INDEX

ABOUT THE AUTHOR

Jim Lockard is an ordained minister with the International Centers for Spiritual Living. He leads a warm and welcoming spiritual community, the Center for Spiritual Living, Simi Valley in California. His ministry began in 1995 in Fort Lauderdale, Florida. He speaks throughout North America on a variety of spiritual and human potential topics, and presents spiritual workshops in beautiful locations around the world.

Prior to his entry into the ministry, he served as a law enforcement officer in Maryland and Dade County, Florida for 24 years. During that time, he authored the book *SURVIVAL THINKING* (Charles C. Thomas, Publishers, 1991), which deals with the psychology of human performance as applied to public safety professionals. He sees *SACRED THINKING* as a natural progression in consciousness from his earlier work.

Jim lives in Oak Park, California with his wife, Dorianne and step-daughter, Grace Stauffer. His daughter, Heather, lives and works in New York.

You can connect with Jim on www.Facebook.com and at **www.SacredThinking.com** Visit www.SacredThinking.com for information about SACRED THINKING and to purchase *I EXPAND THE INFINATE*, Jim's CD of prayer set to the beautiful music of Robert Hitz.

NOTES:

NOTES:

NOTES: